THE
GREATEST
SEMESTER
EVER

THE
GREATEST SEMESTER EVER

A Memoir of Studying Abroad

Michael Sean McEVILLY

ARPress
ILLUMINATING IDEAS
EMPOWERING VOICES

ARPress
45 Dan Road Suite 5
Canton, MA 02021

Hotline: 1(888) 821-0229
Fax: 1(508) 545-7580

Ordering Information:
Quantity sales. Special discounts are available on quantity purchases by corporations, associations, and others. For details, contact the publisher at the address above.

Printed in the United States of America.

ISBN-13:   Softcover   979-8-89330-058-1
             eBook   979-8-89330-059-8

Library of Congress Control Number: 2024901185

CONTENTS

DEDICATION

To my father, Michael T. McEvily, without whose coaxing and lobbying on my behalf, my journeys never would have materialized. And as his brother, Uncle Pa (Patrick), described it, "You're 21 years old, and you've got the Devil by the tail!"

1 - Prelude to Flight

If you want to do something amazing, see something amazing, or even achieve your wildest dreams, you're going to have to go beyond the horizon and venture into the unknown. While the pomp in that sounds glorious, fluffy, and boisterous, the reality is that it's true. You'll never see the world by staying in "Mayberry".

The thought of studying in Europe started long before January of 1989. The study abroad program at our College was still in its infancy, and there were ads all over campus advertising for it. I was already well traveled internationally by this time. My dad was from Co. Mayo, Ireland, and mom was from Chicago of Irish-born parents, so we were about as Irish as it got. Prior to this semester, I had been to Ireland 5 times and England twice, so I knew my way around somewhat already.

I had to convince my parents first that studying in Europe would be a good idea. That wasn't easy. Dad, on the other hand, was all for it. Afterall, he left his home in Ireland at the age of 18 years to make a new life for himself and his future family in America. He thought it would be a great adventure, and endless opportunities to learn about yourself, the world, and of course, academics from another point of view. Mom wasn't so easy to convince though. She's more the timid and reserved type. She's not the one to set out onto an Odyssey into the unknown. She's more cautious.

Part of convincing mom was to come up with the funding I would need to survive while overseas. During the summer of 1988, I worked for a temp agency and they found me a job working at O'Hare International on the building of Terminal 1, the United Airlines Terminal. We worked with United's computer technicians refurbishing used computer terminals from Denver's old Stapleton International which was closing down. Nice, they were building a brand new state-of-the-art terminal with used goods to put inside of it. Oh well, it was good work and good, steady pay, and that's exactly what I needed to convince mom to allow me to study abroad.

Now, I had to decide in which country I wanted to study? I liked the idea of Ireland, because I have so much family there, but that could also be a big distraction. I was good with Spanish, because I studied 4.5 years in junior high, high school, and college, but that was basically Spanish I &II done twice. They were easy A's, but I still wasn't ready to study in Spain. It was looking like England was the obvious choice. Hey, what the hell? I love British classic rock bands (or Progressive Rock as they call it). Maybe we'll catch a concert of a famous band?

Once those of us who were committed to study abroad sealed the deal, we had to start organizing and making plans. Kim was a good friend whom I met at our meetings. She also lived on the Northside of Chicago, and we had friends in common from high school which made it an even smaller world. This friend in common, Mary, worked with a guy named Christos Correles

2

originally from Corinth, Greece. Chris, as we called him, was a bit older than us, but he had a social streak a mile wide, and he liked to party. It must have been when Kim and I were home at Thanksgiving when we met Chris at a party and made plans. He was going to be home in Corinth during the following Spring, April '89. We'd be roaming Europe at the time, so we decided we'd pay him a visit. This was the original plan, but neither Chris, Kim, nor I could know how many college students would show up on his doorstep. Poor guy.

Well, our semester wasn't entirely in London. We only studied there until March 17th, St. Patrick's Day, and then traveled to the continent. Now, what kind of heathen would make us travel on St. Paddy's Day? None other than Dr. O'Neill our program leader, one would surmise? In all reality though, he was probably trying to avoid the debacle that happened the year before in our Europe Program's initial year. Those students thought it would be a great idea to go over to Dublin for St. Patrick's Day. Unfortunately in the 1980s, St. Paddy's Day was still a "Holy Day of Obligation" in Ireland. There were no parades or big raucous parties like everyone was expecting, and it turned out to be a total flop.

The remainder of our semester would be spent on a study-tour of Paris, Rome, and Florence for about 5-6 days in each city. That was the first and only semester I've ever studied without having to buy books, because the places we were touring were like walking through textbooks themselves. After the study-tour, everyone had Eurail Passes that we all bought back in The States. The pass was open-ended for a month from the date initialized, and it was good for all rail, ferry, and steamer travel in Western Europe excluding Great Britain. That would later prove to be an extreme pain in the ass. Britain was our home base, and we couldn't even use our Eurail Passes either in Britain or to and from across water.

Near the end of the Fall '88 Semester, we had meetings with some kind of organizing committee for what lay in-store in our Spring Semester. This was where we determined our living accommodation assignments. Instead of living in a dorm, we were all assigned to live with host families, so the ideal situation would be if there were two students per English family. However among the guys, there were only 7 of us, so someone was going to have to triple-up. That was me, Bryan and Szyd.

Szyd and Bryan were great guys. I had known Bryan for a long time. We went to Ralph Waldo Emerson Jr. High together, Class of 1982. After junior high, we just lost touch. He went to Maine South High School, and I went to Notre Dame High School. Years later we met again. I think it was in the cafeteria at our College, but it was mind blowing to see someone from way back. The term "way back" being quite relative to the years an individual has already lived at the time.

Szyd was a guy from St. Louis. Very bright and quick on the uptake, but not always likely to let you know right away. We met my sophomore year when he was living in St. Joe's Hall right across from Heffron Hall where I lived. I knew him from the parking lot between our two buildings, and one day I sold him a ticket to one of our fraternity parties, and we've been buds ever since. Like me, he had some family in Europe, but not in the volume of relatives that I had in Ireland. He was planning on visiting his uncle in Belgium after our Eurail Tour.

All that was left to do Stateside was one last road trip to our College of Minnesota to say goodbye to our other classmates and friends that we probably wouldn't see until the next August. O'Hare International was the last stop before our adventure began, and we all met at the departure gate. This was way before TSA or The Department of Homeland Security, so they even had a rollaway bar at the gate just for us and our families who were there to see us off. There were so many scared and nervous parents there. Kim's father, with a tear in his eye, slipped me $20 and asked me to look after his little girl and please walk her home at night. How could I resist when it came to someone who would turn out to be a lifelong friend?! Despite all of the nervousness and apprehension, I was about as excited as one could be.

2 - NIGHT FLIGHT
Friday 1/20/1989

C oming in on final approach to Gatwick, I had my Walkman headphones on for effect. Of course, I was listening to Led Zeppelin's Night Flight because the lyrics just seemed to be quite appropriate. "So I said good-bye to all my friends and packed my hopes inside a matchbox, because I know it's time to fly."

We finally arrived after being delayed in Chicago for three hours waiting for a damned fuel gauge to be flown in from St. Louis. The worst part was that it was an international flight, therefore we could not disembark because Customs already processed us. We were stuck at the gate on the plane and we couldn't do a thing. We were flying TWA based out of St. Louis as opposed to one of the many carriers that call Chicago home. I guess you get what you pay for? They must have been the low cost carrier?

Nobody really knew exactly what or where to go when we got off the plane, but we managed to find Dr. O'Neill, of our College in Minnesota, who met us with Dr. Hugh Papworth, of West London Institute which was our new school away from school.

We loaded our bags onto the coach and drove to West London's Lancaster House Campus in Isleworth, London. There, we met up with Dr. Jean Edwards who was the other professor dedicated to our London Experience along with Dr. Papworth.

Because of the aviation mishaps, Dr. Papworth and Dr. Edwards made trips driving everyone to the host families. All except Rose and Andie. Their host family wasn't home so they came with Szyd, Bryan, and me to the Kent's house for tea.

We lived with the Kent family right around the corner from the Lancaster House Campus at 8 Grove Rd., Isleworth, Middlesex, England. What a place?! It was a detached home in London which is very rare and expensive. Mr. Kent, who was a professor of Die-Casting at Hounslow Community College, bought this house in 1967 for £5,000, and now it was worth a million pounds in 1989 currency.

Alicia, Mr. and Mrs. Kent in their proper English garden

Well, we visited for hours with Rose, Andie, us and the Kent's until Rose and Andie's "British mom" came to pick them up.

At dinner, we all had a prelude to what we figured was going to be a weight gaining experience. Mrs. Kent was a wonderful cook in addition to being a great hostess and the nicest person that you could meet during a long walk on a Sunday afternoon. Despite the rough start to this trip, things are beginning to really look up.

After dinner, we unpacked and decided the best way to fight jet-lag was to fight sleep and go out boozing. Go to sleep at the same time Londoners do, and we'll wake up at the same time they do. Thus defeating jet-lag. Mr. Kent told us of a pub called the London Apprentice. His daughter, Alicia, who was our age, 21, took us there and to another place called the Town Wharf where for some reason you have to be 21 to enter. The drinking age in Britain and throughout Europe is 18, but I guess this place didn't want the younger, less mature drinkers there. It did seem like an affluent neighborhood.

I think this was the place that Mr. Kent said that Henry VIII used to stop for a pint on his way from London to his palace at Hampton Court. It was an interesting night for drinks. We ended up having only about 4 pints total that night, and no two were the same. It was unusual because regular beer drinkers just stick to one flavor. They don't do the mix and match form or drinking. Maybe it was a way of finding a new flavor for London after the swill we'd been drinking in Minnesota. Mixing many different beers will have a tendency to give you a hangover.

Saturday 1/21/1989

We woke up the next morning feeling pretty good after a night's rest. We had breakfast and Rose and Andrea came to our house.

Then we were to meet Dr. O'Neill at the Osterley stop on the Piccadilly Line of the famous London Underground. They also call it The Tube, and this stop would become "home" to us in the coming months. Dr. O'Neill showed us how to buy a "Day Pass" for the tubes and buses. For £2.30, you could go all over London on public transportation for the day.

There were 26 of us in our class from our College in Minnesota. We all took the Tube into central London and got off at Leicester Square on our way to the American Express Office so people could change money. What traveling amateurs?! Before I left Chicago, I went downtown to a British bank to get my travelers cheques in British Pounds. After all, I planned on being in London for at least 6 months. More locations in London, a stronger currency, and NO FEES every time I have to get money. I got even luckier when I found that Barclay's Bank had a location at the bottom of our street from the Kent's house.

After the American Express excursion, some of us decided we wanted to lose the big crowd and see some of London on our own. Szyd, Bryan, Kim, Chrissy, Julie, Kelly, Cheryl, and I bailed on the crowd at Trafalgar Square. Down one of the streets, I noticed Buckingham Palace, and off we were. London was our own to discover! On our tour, we saw Big Ben, Parliament, Westminster Abbey, and the rest of the neighborhood in the Westminster area of London.

We had lunch at an American pizza joint which was apparently pretty good. We heard about Punch and Judy's in Covent Garden and went on a quest. En route, we saw an hysterical street entertainer who fooled a blindfolded volunteer thinking he was throwing knives at him while another guy was sticking them in the styrofoam next to his head and his crotch.

9

We eventually found Punch and Judy's which is a 200 year old pub in Covent Garden. We only had a couple of pints and went to catch the Tube at the Covent Garden Station to go home for dinner. Mrs. Kent's cooking is not something to be late for.

At dinner, Mr. Kent told us that Rose must have gotten separated from the rest of the crowd and couldn't find her way back to her host family's house. She wandered around for about 2 hours not knowing where she was, which had to be frightening. She could, though, remember where our house was because we were right around the corner from the Lancaster House Campus, and she eventually went to knock on the door. Mr. Kent drove her home.

That night, everyone went to the London Apprentice Pub which Mr. Kent recommended last night. It was like a Yankee Invasion. With 26 of us, give or take, we took over. Later, we heard of a late night disco in Richmond and went. We were turned away at the door. The place was supposedly packed and besides, we didn't have proper attire. The bouncer was an asshole anyway, so we caught the LAST bus back and went home.

Sunday 1/22/1989

We slept until 1pm. My problem was that I forgot to wind my alarm clock. Every time I woke up and looked over, I thought it was 7am. Duh! As a result we had lunch at 1:30pm. This was an early slight faux pas. Part of the deal between our College and the host families was that the families would provide breakfast and dinner for the students. As far as lunch was concerned, we were on our own. Now here we were in our second day eating at 1:30 in the afternoon. Did I mention that the Kent's, although

10

the most hospitable, friendly, and adorable people you could meet, are a very PROPER English family and like to adhere to the rules. This will arise as a slight issue later again after we meet Ijaz and Riaz.

After lunch, Mr. Kent, his daughter Alicia, Szyd, Bryan, and I packed into their car to go see Hampton Court which was built by Henry VIII as his country palace. Quite the impressive abode! This was the place Henry was going to when he stopped at that pub The Town Wharf that we went to on our first night. This was one of the reasons we were so lucky to be placed with the Kents. They were so proud of their home of Isleworth, London, England, and Mr. Kent was such the consummate educator that they wanted to share all that they had with the world. And, quite a bit they did have to share.

After dinner, I hadn't yet completed my Cathedral paper, so I got moving right away. SuperBowl XXIII was on that night and we were all going out to an American place in Richmond called MacArthur's. I wasn't finished by the time Bryan and Szyd were leaving, so I just met them there later. I finally finished typing on Mr. Kent's computer (another perk of living with the Kents), and Alicia helped me print it out. Then I took the bus to Richmond and got there by half-time which was about 11pm. Normally, pubs would have all been closed, but because MacArthur's was an American place, the local magistrate gave them an exemption until the game was over. We drank loads of Budweiser, because of the restaurant's American theme. Yuck! Our tab was about £100 which was about $1.75 to a pound, so we racked up $175 worth of drink, and we hadn't even hit our first class yet.

We called a cab because it was so late that even the buses stopped running.

Once we got within a few blocks of the Kent's house, we had one of those "It seemed like a good idea at the time" kind of moments. We actually tried to ditch the cab. Bryan and Szyd went one way around the corner, and I ran up the street thinking I'd duck between two houses, out the back, and on my way. WRONG!! Most of the houses in England are built together. They're all connected! There was no ducking between houses tonight!

Well, I had run out of steam, and the cab driver decided to follow me instead of Bryan and Szyd. I walked along the street because I couldn't run anymore while the cabbie kept warning me that he was calling the police. A block or so down, there was an apartment high-rise with a driveway that went around back on one side of the building. I took off running again after catching my breath, ran behind the cab, and up the driveway toward the back of the building. The cab followed me as planned. When the cab was hemmed in with the only way out being the one he just drove in, I continued running around the back of the building, back out to the street and out of his line of sight. Around the next corner, I dove under a bush and waited for the coast to clear. After a few moments, two people came walking along. It was Bryan and Szyd, and we scared the shit out of each other. That was the last time we tried a stunt like that.

3 - WE GOTTA GO TO SCHOOL, AFTERALL
Monday 1/23

We left for class at the Gordon House Campus of West London Institute about 8:30 am. It was only about a half-mile walk from the Lancaster House Campus which is where we first congregated.

Our first day was only an orientation in the morning. People weren't feeling too bad when they got to class, but as time wore on, hangovers began to set in. Before long, everyone was feeling like "death warmed over".

For the whole semester, we're on our own for lunch. Our host families only provide breakfast and dinner. The most cost effective place to have lunch in London is the pub. It's where all the locals go. Lunchtime in London can often resemble Happy Hour.

On our first day, we had lunch at a pub which was at the bottom of our street called the Iron Bridge. Not too creative of a name though. There was an iron train bridge going overhead. There was also a Newsagent Shop right next door where they put out the day's news publications in a rack outside the door. We learned early that The Sun newspaper had a columnist on page 3 that had trouble getting people to read his column. His solution was to publish everyday, right next to his column, a photo of a topless girl! Well, we never bought the newspaper, but we did stop each day to get a glimpse of The Page 3 Girl.

I only had a small sandwich because I was one hurting puppy after the Budweiser we had the night before while watching SuperBowl XXIII. I don't like Budweiser in America as it is, but in England it was everywhere and stronger so it can just give you a worse hangover. Getting back to the Kent's house about 3am wasn't really helping matters either.

That night, we were supposed to have an "Introduction to the U.K." lecture. Well, nobody told the instructor so he never showed up. Instead, the whole class, including Dr. Papworth, went over to the campus pub for a pint. He was a very generous man, and he bought all of us a drink.

We then had a major game of Quarters. Silly drinking games are a good icebreaker and way to meet your fellow students. We were also partying with some rugby players, and those guys are crazy! Two of them were stripping on the table down to their jockstraps in what I interpreted as some kind of Initiation Ritual using hazing. Who was getting hazed here, them or us?

Tuesday 1/24

The next morning was easy because we only had to walk to Lancaster House which was around the corner and up the street. The class of the day was Geology & Scenery with Dr. Mark Sleep. He was a pretty cool and on-the-level kind of professor. He had a really unique way of explaining how to keep stalactites and stalagmites separate in your mind. He said to think of Mites. They're little bugs that crawl around on the ground, therefore stalagmites start low and grow upwards. On the other hand, he addressed the male students in particular saying, "Lads, tights are meant to come DOWN". Stalactites come down from above.

That lasted until noon, and we went back to The Iron Bridge for lunch. Today it was just Bryan, Szyd, Dan, and myself. After lunch, the four of us went back to central London. Bryan needed some good walking shoes, and besides, we wanted to see the town.

Dan knew where the famed, or infamous, Soho area was, so we checked it out. That place was unreal! It kinda made Rush St. look like Kiddieland even though everyone told us that it had been cleaned up a lot.

Dinner with the Kents was always a nice and usually memorable experience. Besides getting a top notch meal with a nice dessert, we could always count on the arrival of The British Airways

Concorde arriving from New York at 6pm. Even the crystal pieces on display would shake as you could feel the whole house vibrate. This happened two times a day everyday. At 6pm and 9pm the Concorde would make the whole house rattle because we were right in the flight path for Heathrow. If you were outside and looked up, you could see the markings on the fuselage. Well, that's what you get when you can fly between New York and London in only 3 hours.

After dinner, we worked on our journals a bit, and then went up to the campus pub. We met up with Paul, Dan, and some of our new English classmates–Ijaz Bhatti, his brother Riaz, and their other flatmate Michelle. We met them the night that the rugby initiates were being hazed. Ijaz and I were sitting close to each other and had some sort of jovial interaction. I noticed that he bore a striking resemblance to Steve Perry, the lead singer from Journey, and I mentioned it to him. He said yes that he had heard that before. After that we started talking all about both British and American rock & roll and found out we were peas in a pod. It turns out that their flat was just right around the corner from the Kent's house, so we went back for tea. This flat will turn out to be our after-hours party house.

Ijaz, their flat-mate Michelle, and Riaz. Don't mind the Lenin poster. They weren't really Communists. Just rebellious.

Ijaz Bhatti was older than Riaz, but Riaz was the bigger of the two. He kind of looked like a rugby player. They came from an interesting background too. Their mother was from Germany, their father was from Pakistan, and they were both born and raised in Southampton, England along the south coast. I guess I could also relate to them being the son of immigrants to a new country.

That night we were introduced to "hot knives" which would have a very positive effect on our European college experience. We found our "connection"! British college students don't smoke buds like Americans do. They get hashish, mostly Black Moroccan Hash, so we needed to learn a new way of smoking. Our new friends put the tips of two butter knives in the flame of the gas stove until they glowed red. Then, tap a pre-rolled up little ball of hash which will stick to the knife. Using a 2 liter

Coke bottle with the bottom cut off, stick the knives in the bottle and sear the ball of hash. It instantly carbonizes and fills the bottle with smoke. Just inhale from the bottle opening and float away… Next school year when we were back in Minnesota, we figured out it doesn't work on an electric stove. Oh well.

Wednesday 1/25

Today was the busiest day of the week. We had British Architecture and Landscape with Bryan Seagrove in the morning. He was a refined and mellow guy. Nonetheless, the class was pretty cool. With a class like this, your textbook is the world around you. Living in London is like walking through the pages of a history book. It's very cool.

Again, we had lunch at the Iron Bridge because we had another class at 1:30pm and didn't have the time to look around for another pub with good food.

The afternoon class was Geography of London with Mike Turner. He was the Instructor that blew us off on Monday night. He was a cool guy though, and the class was pretty fun. This was also the guy who would later turn us on to the Indian fast food of Samosas. Delicious. He showed us the London that's a little off the beaten path. "City skills" that would prove invaluable during our time there.

We had our proper dinner and then right out the door to see the comedy "Lettuce & Lovage" at The Globe Theatre located between Piccadilly Circus and Leicester Square. This would become our normal Wednesday night gig for British Theatre class. What a class?! Every Wednesday evening, we would meet at a different theater in the West End and see the latest performances that London had to offer. We met once at midterm to turn in a written review of what we had seen, and we did the same again for the final. Great class!

Although on this night, the first act of "Lettice and Lovage" was lacking a little bit. It was too long and drawn out, but the next two acts were really good. The acting was superb.

After the show, we went around the corner to The White Horse Pub. There, they had one of those "new-fangled" CD Jukeboxes, and we heard some of the best music we've heard since we arrived in England...besides what I listen to when I'm pounding the pavement walking all over town. British Classic Rock sounds really cool when you're walking through a "history book" like London, but they call it Progressive Rock which is fine with me.

Thursday 1/26

I only had one class today. It was in the morning, so I had to wake up early while Bryan and Szyd slept in. They only had one class too, but it was in the afternoon.

My sole class that day was Contemporary British Authors with Patricia Owen. I had an ominous feeling that this class was going to require more work than any other. My first clue was that the class lasted the entire time period. British professors seem to be fairly loose when it comes to the timeclock except for Patricia Owen.

We got lunch at a new place today. We went to The George. These English pubs really don't put a lot of effort into naming their places of business. Then again, it could be because many, if not most, of the English pubs are corporately owned, and the proprietor is merely what we'd call a franchisee. Nonetheless, The George was a nice reasonably priced place.

I was free all afternoon, so I took a long bath and caught up on my journal. The Kents had a bathtub and not a shower because of the American fascination with standing in the shower way too long. They used to have one, but the water bill went through the roof with previous American exchange students. I couldn't blame them.

Before dinner, I walked up to Lancaster House to see if Dan and Paul were up there shooting hoops, but I didn't see them. I walked to Ijaz's flat to hang out and make plans for the night. I found out the bartenders at the Lancaster House Pub were on strike because of being understaffed for the Wednesday night discos.

Instead, we went to a place called Chequers to booze it up. We played another drinking game called Mexican which is played with a cup and a pair of dice. We played for a few hours and had a wild time. When we left, some of our classmates started their collections of pint glasses. It's not like we don't have them in America?

Friday 1/27

Today, we met Kim, Kelly, and Cheryl at the bus stop at the bottom of the street. We were going to go shopping in Richmond first, and then meet Jeanne at the Tube stop. We were going to go see some museums, but things went awry. We just ended up shopping all day.

We had lunch at an Italian restaurant that had all you can eat spaghetti for £ 2.95. We learned to take advantage of deals like that whenever we could.

Shopping for me consisted of buying a new brush, because my hair was getting too long and bushy for just a comb. We, of course, had to stop for 2 pints at some out-of-the-way pub, real "salt of the earth" kind of stuff.

We walked back to Isleworth via the footbridge behind the Gordon House Campus, which we returned to later that night for the Disco. At the Disco, we sat in the Maria Grey Lounge playing Quarters for a while until the bar closed at 10:30pm. It was only then that we went into the dancing room to see how that was doing. WRONG!! The music, if you could call it that, was horrible. So, we finished our drinks and left. Naturally, we finished the night with "tea" at Ijaz's flat.

Saturday 1/28

Today was the weekend trip to Oxford. Our program brought us on several field trips which were very cool. Like I said, walking through England is like walking through a history book with the best live animation.

Our bus left a little after 9:30 am. The day was pissing rain almost the whole day, so it was rather miserable. We got to Oxford about 10:30am and had a half hour to kill before our tour began. It turned out to be an agonizingly long 2 hour tour with a whispering tour guide that I couldn't hear two words from. For some reason, I expected more out of the world acclaimed Oxford University. Oh well.

We had 3 hours to kill before our bus left for London at 4pm. There was a lot of down time on this excursion. We first went to have a pub lunch at the White Horse Pub, and then we did a bit of shopping. I think I've done more shopping in this past week than I have all last semester!

We finished off our spare time with what else? A few pints. This wasn't necessarily the best decision for me because my bladder barely made it back to Isleworth.

That night, Szyd, Bryan, Alicia, Mr. Kent, and I went out to a couple of very old, very nice pubs. One was called The Dove which was known for having many famous patrons, and the other was called The City Barge which faced the River Thames.

Mr. Kent went home early on the bus, but Alicia stayed with us and we all drove home after close.

4 - LEARNING THE ROPES
Sunday 1/29

One of my sisters had a boyfriend named Mick who was from Co. Clare, Ireland and was visiting his home at Christmas time. He was on his way back to Chicago via London when he got stranded there after a British Customs Agent tore up Mick's legally obtained visa right in front of him. "Paddy" as the British refer to the Irish is a second class citizen in England, and the Customs Agent didn't believe it was real. All he could do was order a replacement from the American Embassy, but that takes time. So, he bunked up with some of his cousins who lived in London, and found some day-work laboring to stay afloat financially until he could get back to Chicago.

So, my sister, Maureen, gave me a phone number where I could contact Mick. I woke up at 10am and gave him a ring. I was going to meet him at a place called The Swan in Stockwell in south London. It was a little bit of a distance from Isleworth, but I wasn't fazed. An Irish Pub with live Irish music promised to be a great time.

Mr. Kent asked me what part of London I was going to, and I told him Stockwell. He was taken aback slightly because that's not the nicest part of town. I realized that when I changed from the Piccadilly Line on the Underground to the Victoria Line. As the Victoria Line went farther south, I started to realize that I was the only white person left on the train. It felt like I was back in Chicago. I walked out of the Underground cautiously with my eyes everywhere watching out. When I got up to the street, I was relieved to see The Swan directly across the street.

They had great Irish Music at The Swan. Such a diamond in the rough. A nice Irish Pub in the middle of a dodgy south London neighborhood. I met a couple of Mick's cousins and some other friends. We drank and sang until the place closed at 3pm. Drinking on a Sunday in Britain is complicated. The pub opens early, but closes at 3pm and reopens at 7pm. The whole idea behind it is to force the men to go home to their families for dinner, then they can go back to the pub later.

We got a bite to eat, and then hung out at Maggie's flat in Morden. She's one of Mick's cousins. On the way back to The Swan, we stopped at another one of Mick's cousin's flat's for tea. Back at The Swan, we drank and sang until after close. The only problem with that was that the Underground stopped running, and I couldn't get home. So, Mick, his other cousin John and I stayed at Maggie's flat for the night.

That was the night I shared a twin bed with my future brother-in-law.

Monday 1/30

We woke up at about 7am, and Mick, John, and myself took the bus to the Morden Underground stop. Of course in our hungover states, we got on the wrong train. Once we realized, those two got onto a different line and went to work. I flip flopped back and caught the right one. I changed onto the Piccadilly Line in the Underground and finally got home by 9:30am. I think the Kents are beginning to wonder whether I'm actually a "good boy" or not? Do I have a hidden "bad boy" side that I mask with good manners? I guess we'll see.

Bryan and Szyd were still sleeping, so we didn't wake them. They must not have had class that morning. Mrs. Kent was visiting with her brother, James, who was home visiting from Johannesburg, South Africa. He was a scientist of some sort. He was also a very active man. We went skiing in Uxbridge in northwestern London. They actually had an artificial slope that was made out of bristle brush material. Not quite like the real thing, but it was fun nonetheless. Until we walked home.

I can't remember why, exactly, we walked home, but we did. I was still new to London, so I didn't yet have an accurate perspective of where I was. On the other hand, James grew up in London so I trusted him. The trip from Uxbridge was on a spur line of the Piccadilly Line. To take that home, we'd have to go into the city to the main Piccadilly Line and back out again to the Osterley stop where we lived, so maybe that's why we walked instead. He must have forgotten distances in his hometown, because we walked for hours. That was after artificial skiing, so my legs were cashed out when we got home. I've probably walked in London so far more than I did in the last semester in Minnesota.

That night's lecture was by a Bozo impersonator named Martin Folly. His lecture had the unbelievably condescending title of "The Irish Question". Did this guy not realize who we were? We might be Americans and come from a predominantly Protestant country, but there's a lot of Irish Catholic-Americans among us, and we don't like being alluded to as though we were lowly second-class citizens that need to be "managed or re-educated" by the wisdom of the British Government.

I couldn't resist. Martin Folly was just like his name suggests, was pure folly. He was an ass who only told half of the story about the Troubles in Northern Ireland. He only lectured from the point of view of the Protestants and the British. No consideration for the opposing Irish Catholic point of view, so I felt obligated to assist him with facts that he left out. Boy, did this guy and I get into it. I could tell I derailed the whole lecture he had planned to propagandize American college students. Up the rebels! As they would say in Ireland.

After class, we all went to the campus pub, and Dr. Papworth, one of the English professors dedicated to our group, came chasing after me. I thought, at first, that I was in some kind of trouble, but he was genuinely curious about where I learned all of the facts I spouted about the history of The Troubles and wanted to learn. We had a really good conversation, and he told me that he's never heard a lot of what I said. It was then, as a Mass Communications major, that I realized Britain does NOT have a truly free press. There's too much governmental influence in how the British media disseminate the news. This was a college professor who didn't even know the truth about The Troubles.

It was also Jeanne's birthday, so we celebrated that too while we were at the pub. After the pub, we of course, went back to Ijaz's flat for a "Topper".

Tuesday 1/31

Today was Geology class again. Nothing really stood out. It's all about British geology, but on the upside, we will be going on a field trip to Swansea, Wales in February. This trip would prove to be very "revealing" about our good professor. But, that's another story.

For lunch, we again went to The George. Bryan, Kelly, Cheryl, Karen, Kim, and I went together, and I'm starting to wonder what the local pub proprietors think of this American invasion on their neighborhood? We were starting to get familiar with places for lunch.

After lunch, we all had our one-on-one meetings with Dr. O'Neill. I'm not really fond of Dr. O'Neill, but we have a professional relationship. I guess he's also trying to baby-sit us to one degree or another. Now it was home for a nap.

That night, Bryan, Cheryl, Kelly, and I went to Ijaz's flat. We hung out there having a few beers, usually just "chewing the fat" about either music or how Americans and Brits are two peoples separated by a common language. I think Ijaz had a TV, but he never put it on when company was over because it killed conversation.

A little later, Ijaz and his brother Riaz had some friends over for a little party. We were doing our normal thing, just drinking beers, smoking hot-knives, and listening to "progressive rock" as they called it.

The party was going great until this one English chick piped up and got all uppity where Americans were concerned. She started telling me how Americans have no history or culture and that is why they invade Britain every year during tourist season because they're starved for culture and history. She referred to us as "The Colonies", and that's when the niceties were over.

This girl was drunk and out of line, not to mention a little out-classed. I normally defer from having an intellectual battle with an unarmed person, but this time, I couldn't resist. She insisted that we pronounced Vincent Van Gogh's name wrong (he used to live in our neighborhood so it was sensitive). The English say Van "Goff" whereas Americans say Van "Go". She insisted that the "gh" consonant combination in English made an "F" sound. Although sometimes it does, I had to remind her of the likes of "might, flight, and fight" where the "gh" consonant is not even pronounced as in Vincent Van Gogh's name. As long as I was at it, I reminded her that Britain stopped teaching "structural grammar" (according to Ijaz) in 1973 out of a fear of restricting literary creativity, so who the hell was she to tell me anything about the mechanics of the English language. Well, she was about to erupt, so I thought I'd help her along. She screamed at me, "Don't you know the Queen's English?" Laughingly, I responded, "I hope to God she is!" The other guys had to save me from being attacked, but I was feeling good.

We then went up to the Lancaster House pub for a few more pints, and to socialize with some other people. As the night went on, all this partying gave us the munchies, so we went to a late-night fast food place called American Dream. It was a burger joint run by some Chinese guys. We took the food back to Ijaz's flat because, after all, it's still January, and they sold food through a walk-up window on the street. I had a chili burger that was so unbelievably hot, I could barely eat it.

We hung out for a while longer, then Bryan and I walked the girls home.

Wednesday 2/1

Again, we are at our busiest day of the week, because every Wednesday evening, we have tickets to live shows in London's West End. I'm tellin' ya', British Theatre class is awesome!!

This morning, we had British Architecture class with Bryan Seagrove. This class is going to meet at different locations around town for in-depth sightseeing for the next two weeks. Today's meeting place was the Westminster stop on the Underground. From there we went out to explore the neighborhood we explored on our own on our first Saturday, but this time we had an instructor from West London Institute as our own personal tour guide. This is what I meant by saying walking through London is like walking through a history book.

We quickly chowed at McDonald's for lunch today, and rushed back to Lancaster House for Geography class. This is also a class that will often meet at various locations around town. London is our textbook and classroom!

Scarfing down dinner, or any meal, on Wednesdays had become the norm. After dinner, we had to race back to Leicester Square to see the play "Les Liaison Dangereuse" or Dangerous Liaisons in English. The play was great! Theater in the West End is second to none!

We had a pint next door afterwards, and then went home exhausted. By the time we got back to Isleworth, I had gotten a second wind, so I went over to Ijaz and Riaz's flat to "unlax and rewind". Then I went to bed.

Thursday 2/2

Today, we woke up early to hit the Museum of London to research our term-paper for British Museums class. The Museum of London is a chronological history of London from 4000 B.C. to the present. It basically covers the whole kit and kaboodle, so there was endless material to write a paper.

Not knowing our way around central London too well yet, we spent way too long walking around looking for a good deal on lunch. We ended up trying a sandwich shop. I hesitate to call it a proper deli, because I had a French bread with two slices of roast beef and tomato slices the size of quarters.

Our afternoon class was Art in British Museums. We met at The National Gallery and took a tour of that place. Afterwards, we went next door to The National Portrait Gallery. I wasn't too impressed. First of all, I had had my fill of museums for the day, and secondly, it was like walking through a magazine of famous and semi-famous people. More than likely, a few infamous people too. Big deal.

After dinner, we all caught up on a few things. Later, Szyd and I stopped by to pick up Ijaz and Riaz, and we went up to the Lancaster House pub to meet some people. Bryan and Cheryl and a few others came out. While at the pub, we discovered all of the weird flavors of crisps (potato chips) like sausage, chicken and a few other way-off things.

Before we went to bed, we stopped over at Ijaz and Riaz's flat for a "cup of tea" and went home.

5 - DINNER WITH BREEGE AND STEVE

Breege is one of my first cousins from Westport in Co. Mayo, Ireland. She lived in London at the time with her husband Steve, who is also an Irishman from Co. Laois. They lived in the Southgate neighborhood of north central London. It was the third stop from the end of the Piccadilly Line on the Underground at the opposite end of where I was living. It was a long way away. It was like a road-trip on an urban commuter rail. London is really big!

Breege and Steve had a lovely house on Arlington Rd. where I would later live after the semester was done. Everyone else would go back to America after they traveled around following the semester's end. I wanted to stretch it out for as long as I could, so I used the maximum stay on my airline ticket which was 6 months. I didn't return to Chicago until July. Steve worked with legal contracts in the construction business, so he talked to some people and got me a job working as a carpenter on a jobsite building an industrial park. It was great work. I only wish I could have stayed longer.

Anyway, I had been in touch with Breege and Steve, and they invited me over to their house for dinner. My other cousin

Fidelma, Breege's sister, would also be there for dinner. The only problem was that I was REALLY late! That afternoon, our American and English classmates decided to have an afternoon of international sports. We'd teach them how to play American football, and they would later teach us how to play rugby. In retrospect, it probably wasn't a good idea. We played too late, I was grungy, needed a bath, and my calves were totally tightened up. After I bathed, I hobbled to our Tube stop (a.k.a. The Underground) at Osterley for the long journey to Southgate.

By the time I arrived in Southgate, Steve was there waiting for me outside the Tube stop. I was so embarrassed, because I was over an hour late. If he or Breege slapped me upside my head, I wouldn't have blamed them. Breege was wonderful to be able to keep dinner warm all that time. It was still delicious, but what was even more momentous was that Breege got me to eat broccoli for the first time in my life! I hated broccoli. I wouldn't touch it. But, she prepared it with a white cheese sauce. This was incredible! I knew that broccoli was good for me, and I probably needed to eat it, but I just couldn't choke it down on its own. When Breege poured a cheese sauce on top of it, it changed my world of vegetables. I am now a healthy eater to this day thanks to her.

After dinner, we all went out to a local pub called The Southgate. This place would become a staple of our social lives after the semester and touring was done and I lived with them. The proprietor was an Irishman, so all the local Irish hung out there. It was the place where we felt welcome. There, we met up with some people I knew from back in my father's village in Ireland. Some of these folks were my cousin's cousins from the other side of their family. In other words, my father was a brother to Breege and Fidlema's mother, and Michael Grady was their first cousin on their father's side. I'm telling ya', when you come from a big Irish Catholic family, you learn how to sort out the who, what, when, where, why, and we already know the how, so we don't discuss that publicly.

It was such a long way from Southgate to Osterley on the Piccadilly Line that I just stayed over with Breege and Steve. In the morning, I did the classic college "walk of shame" all the way home with nasty bed-head. Ah, who the hell cared. I didn't know anybody anyway.

6 - Guys Night Out in Central London

Of the 26 of us students, there were 7 males and 19 females. We mostly did a lot of co-mingling, but someone came up with the idea of a guys night out. It sounded like a good idea at the time, but before the night would be out, we'd have our first encounter with "Johnny Law", or the "Bobbies" in England. The British police are called "Bobbies" because the founder of Britain's professional police force was named Robert Peale.

Anyway, we all met at Ijaz and Riaz's flat. Of course we had some "gear" as they called it, or hashish. After a few "hot knives" and a couple of beers from the off-license store (the liquor/beer store), we were ready to go on the town. We all walked up to the Osterley stop on the Underground and into central London.

Somehow, we ended up at this classic old pub somewhere in between Covent Garden and Piccadilly Circus. It was a bit out of the way. After a while, we wanted to have another smoke of hashish. I had the "gear" with me so what the hell? Although, we didn't have anything to smoke it out of. So, my inner MacGyver flared, and I grabbed an empty aluminum beer can, dented it for a bowl, and poked little holes in the bowl to act as a screen. Now, we needed a place to do this.

The streets in London are small to begin with, because they all used to be horse cart paths at one time. The farther off the beaten path you go, the smaller the street becomes, and we were off the beaten path. We walked about a block down and saw an alley through to another street, but halfway through there was a dead-end T-junction alley as well. We decided to hide in that little T-junction and smoke a bowl.

Everything was going well until we finished and were leaving the secluded alley. I came out of the T-junction and there were Bobbies who just pulled up on the street to the left. We went right. As we walked down to the street we came in from, we noticed other Bobbies on foot coming up the street and over the fences. Holy shit, we were surrounded. I was holding the hash, so I needed to think quickly. I was walking past a parked car so I bent down, and acting like I was scratching my ankle, threw the little matchbox in which I stored the hash under that car and behind the tire.

The Bobbies finally closed in and corralled us up against the wall, all of us spread eagle. The other guys knew I was carrying the hash and we all worried that we'd all end up in an English jail. While my arms were on the wall, I leaned forward and gave a signal smile to all the guys letting them know I got rid of it. Then everyone could relax and just deal with the search. They had us take off our jackets and searched them along with a thorough pat-down. After a few minutes, they couldn't find anything and gave up. They were really polite for cops too. One was holding out Szyd's jacket to help him put it back on, and Szyd gave him a feared look like "what are you trying to do to me" and held out his hands to catch it. But no, the Bobbie helped him on with his jacket. How nice?

Then one of the Bobbies started documenting the search on a little tablet of paper in triplicate. Bryan thought he was writing us tickets, and said he thought we were free to go? The Bobbies said yes, that he was just making a record of the search which confused us a little.

The Bobbies were kind of confused too with our reactions to them and inquired why. We told them that cops in Chicago wouldn't have been so polite. After searching our jackets, they would have just thrown them back at us, kicked us in the ass, and sent us on our way without even documenting the search. Just then, a couple of Bobbies piped up saying that they should go get jobs in Chicago.

Once everything dispersed, we went back to the same pub we were at before, ordered some pints, and had a seat to kind of decompress and reflect upon what the hell just happened?! I guess my friends didn't even notice me throwing the hash under a car and behind the tire, so I told them the story. A little time had passed, the Bobbies were gone, and I was going after that hash before the car owner moved his car. I walked down the street alone to retrieve it, and it was just where I hoped it would still be! This was incredible! How did we NOT get busted?! They had us, we escaped, and we got our hash back.

There would be a nightcap of hot knives at Ijaz and Riaz's flat that night!

7 – ABERGAVENNY VS. NEWCASTLE-UPON-TYNE

On another free weekend, everyone wanted to go horseback riding in a small Welsh village called Abergavenny. I had been on horseback a number of times before, and although I loved it, I had better things to do. Again, I have family to visit. This time it's cousins on my mom's side called the Potters, no relation to "Harry". They live in Newcastle-upon-Tyne in Northeastern England about 300 miles north of London or roughly a 6 hour road trip on the motorcoach. Well, actually they lived in South Shields which is a suburb of Newcastle, but who outside of Britain has ever heard of South Shields?

My classmates in Abergavenny, Wales. Compliments of Szyd's camera.

Among my relatives, we had my mom's first cousin Kath and her husband Allen. They had three grown children Simon, Mark, and Jane. Jane was my age, and the other two were older than me.

Simon was in the British Merchant Marines and was home at the time I was visiting. He was an English sailor on leave and with a pocket full of money and nothing better to do than watch sports on TV. So, we got up and went into central Newcastle. It was time to meet his mates and party.

To give you an idea of Simon, he was the merchant marine who taught me to drink pints of beer to fight off seasickness five years earlier. It came in handy once on a European ferry, and apparently it works! But, that's another story.

These guys were crazy! If I didn't know better, I'd have guessed that they would have made classic English Soccer Hooligans! Very vehement and emotional about their sport and their bets. And boy, did they bet? Yes! Spring was the beginning of the horse racing season in Britain, and there was a Ladbrokes across the street from the pub we were at which made these lads almost dangerous. Ladbrokes was a bookmaker, or in American vernacular, a legal bookie with a store front. Just like the new ones that have popped up across America. These guys had the racing page of the newspaper spread out on the bar top. One lad came rushing in from the street with a whole stack of betting slips for everyone. I guess the big race was coming close to race time.

They all passed around the betting slips for everyone to fill them out. When they passed some slips to me, I politely refused. I might have had my share of vices, but gambling wasn't one of them. I figured that I worked too hard for my money to just blow it away on a "chance of winning". These guys went silent when they heard me say I didn't bet. These were a bunch of hard partying merchant marines on shore leave. They had pockets full of money after being out to sea, so who of them could imagine not participating in completely Bacchanalian pursuits?

My cousin, Jane, was my age. She was studying to be a nurse like her mother. We went out at night with a group of her friends to show me the riverfront in Newcastle. It was a trendy part of town that had pubs and live music venues as well. As with most British industrial towns, it was rather dirty, but there was a lot of clean-up in progress. It was a great town nonetheless. I kept wondering if I was going to run into Sting, Mark Knopfler from Dire Straits, or Brian Johnson from AC/DC. They're all from Newcastle.

On the way home, Jane and I had to walk through this hilly park that was covered in thick fog that rolled in off of the North Sea. The streetlights were kind of sparse which didn't help matters any. It looked like a scene right out of The Hound of the Baskervilles! That's creepy shit.

My cousins had a caravan in The Lake District, and Jane and I met the rest of them out there via her car. This wasn't a long road trip. It was only about 80-something miles from Newcastle on the east coast to the Lake District on the west coast or the Irish Sea. The road went right along the Scottish-English border, so we pulled over to see an historic site, Hadrian's Wall. It was started in A.D. 122 by the Emperor Hadrian to keep the Picts, the pre-Christian Scots, out of Roman Britain. As astounding of a feat as it might have been to build the wall. There wasn't much there. We kind of just jumped up on top of what was left of the wall and took a photo.

On the way back to London on the motorcoach, I was just listening to my walkman with a Def Leppard tape on full blast. An elderly lady sitting across the aisle from me tapped me on my arm to get my attention. I immediately thought it was too loud for her and instantly apologized. She corrected me by saying that she liked it. Those were her son's mates, or friends, from back in Sheffield. Whoa?! Who was this woman?

As her story went, her son was childhood mates with the band members of Def Leppard. She proceeded to tell me about Rick Savage's struggles as drummer after he lost his arm in a car accident. She knew about how he started using his feet in the hospital bed to tap out a rhythm on the footboard. Then, he worked with engineers to help rig-up gear that would help him play drums without an arm. Whoa?! I couldn't believe a septuagenarian was giving me the insider info on heavy metal! She either read too much Rolling Stone Magazine for a woman her age, or she was telling the truth. Either way, I was flabbergasted.

8 - WALKING HOME FROM HEATHROW

Every Wednesday evening, we had British Theatre class. That meant that we all went to see a wonderful production of whatever was playing in London's West End theater district. It was usually something outstanding by The Royal Shakespeare Company. They didn't just do Shakespeare though, but when they did, you could understand it almost perfectly. A lot had to do with the costuming. They used completely anachronistic costuming so the audience could easily understand who was whom. For example, a villain might be clad in studded biker leathers or a supposedly virtuous character would wear Victorian garb.

A night at the theater was always a pleasant experience, especially since it was in the West End which preceded Broadway's glamor by a long shot. One night during the intermission of a non-Shakespearean play that had "American characters", I mentioned while we were out by the bar that I didn't know there were American actors in the Royal Shakespeare Toupe. A gentleman overheard me and said no, that there were only British actors in the troupe. I was astounded. Their accents were so good that they had me and all of my American classmates fooled.

After the show, we of course had "last call" at the pub down the street before we caught the last Tube out home to Isleworth. On the way out of the pub, there were throngs of people coming out of theaters and pubs all heading for the Tube as well. I got separated from our crowd in the mess and just figured they'd know I know my way home. So, just get to the train, and go home.

It was a cold and rainy night. The day wasn't so bad when we woke up, so I only dressed in a t-shirt and a thick sweater. Big mistake. We were all over the city with our museum classes earlier in the day. By the time the show was over, I was exhausted and cold. The heaters in the Tube are under the upholstered seats, so it's quite comfortable. Maybe too comfortable. I was all alone, and I fell asleep. I woke up looking at a sign for "Terminals 1-5" with an arrow. This was a pure "holy shit" moment! I was the only person left on the train which was parked in the basement somewhere at Heathrow International. Thank God the doors were open so I could get out, and I saw two uniformed Underground workers outside. So, I went to inquire how the hell do I get myself out of this mess?

I scared the shit out of them! I guess they didn't check the train for lost items or people, and certainly didn't expect any lost Yanks to come walking off of the train at some ungodly hour of the night. I was hosed! The next train heading toward London wasn't until 5am, and I wasn't sleeping on the train. Although in retrospect, that might have been the better idea? When I got outside of the underground enclosure where it was dry and warm, I found February's cold rain and wind. I didn't know the surface streets of this town, so all I could do was walk along the M4 motorway for six miles without even a jacket. The motorway is Britain's version of the Interstate Highway System. Very dangerous to walk along, but I had no choice. It was miserable, and I'll never forget it. All I could think was to walk fast and you'll generate body heat. I was like a cold drowned rat when I got back home. Unfortunately, that wouldn't be the last time I fell asleep on the Tube.

9 - AMSTERDAM-THE FIRST TIME

We didn't really have a Spring Break during this semester because it ended by April 2nd. Instead, they gave us a long weekend in February. The big buzz (no pun intended) was that everyone, all 26 wanted to go with Szyd, Bryan, and me to Amsterdam. We had all heard so many stories about Amsterdam, and damn it, we were college students out on the road, so we were going to Party Central!

One of the girls thought it would be cheaper to stay on the island of Great Britain and go visit Edinburgh, Scotland instead. I think they were just afraid of leaving an English speaking country or something like that, because I just couldn't figure out how Edinburgh could be more fun than Amsterdam? Many in our group were still very timid of venturing too far beyond their own personal safe-zone. Whereas, Szyd, Bryan, and I were Gung Ho and wanted to go! We wanted to see everything!

Well, apparently some extensive lobbying took place on behalf of the timid ones wanting to go to Edinburgh instead of Amsterdam. Either way, that didn't faze us. The boys were going to Amsterdam. That is until the timid ones convinced EVERYONE that going to Edinburgh would be better. They even convinced Bryan to go to Edinburgh, but then again, he was having a relationship with one of our classmates, so you can follow where his logical process was going.

Szyd and I stuck with the original plan and went to Amsterdam. The Channel Tunnel or "Chunnel" hadn't been dug yet, so of course, we crossed over on the ferry which took a few hours. On the ferry, we met a few other American college students that we got to know on the crossing. They were on their way to Amsterdam too. We could so easily identify each other as Americans just by what we were wearing. Levi's, Nike, etc. That's why the Canadian college students usually had their flag sewn onto their backpack or jacket to differentiate themselves from Americans. If you heard a Canadian speak and didn't know any better, you ask if they were American. The reply was usually, "Yes, North American". I usually felt embarrassed by my ethnocentrism.

Szyd and I parted with that group from the ferry when we docked at Calais, France, and we made our way overland to Amsterdam via Motorcoach. In our travel Bible, Fodor's Let's Go Europe, there's a list of everything and anything to see or stay everywhere in Western Europe. This was one of our crucial documents that we could NOT have traveled without. Inside, we found a place that just stood out to us. BOB'S YOUTH HOSTEL!! It just called to us, and it was just about a block away from the train station where the motorcoach arrived. We went right there, checked in and crashed out.

The famous Bob's Youth Hostel

At most youth hostels, some kind of breakfast is usually included. At Bob's, it was scrambled eggs, toast, and a cup of tea. The cornerstone of any good way to start your day. It didn't stop there. The students we met on the ferry ended up at Bob's as well. The loud-mouth with glasses stopped me while I was eating and handed me a joint saying, "You're eating too hard. Here, relax for a moment". Whoa?! This town was going to be an adventure.

There was one of Amsterdam's famous coffee shops across the street from Bob's, but we thought better of rushing into the first shop we saw to buy some weed. We didn't know the ropes?

How was it sold? How much did it cost? These all looked like tourist traps, so we took caution in this endeavor. After walking around and asking questions, we found a little place around the corner from Bob's called The Future. We went in and had a seat. When you walk into a coffee shop, they'll naturally hand you a menu. But, this menu lists the house specialty, Marijuana and Hashish. We weren't really interested in any more hash and went with our old standard of buds. The menu listed things like Jamaican, Maui Wowie, Filipino, Thai, the whole nine yards. It was all a standard price of 25 Guilders. What varied was the amount of buds you got depending upon its potency: 2.0g for basic Sensimillia, 1.8g of Jamaican, 1.6g of Thai, etc. Even the napkin holders were interesting. They had an additional little U-shaped compartment to dispense rolling papers. We were in college student heaven!

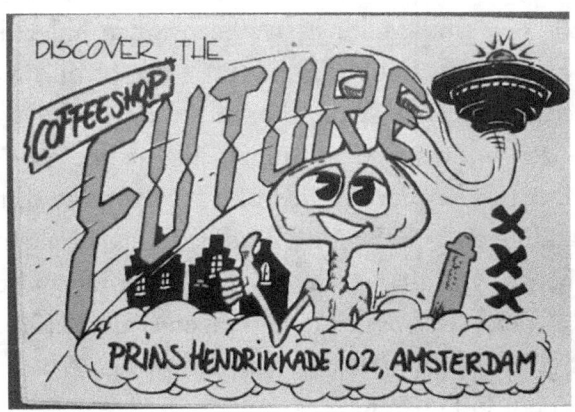

The Future was our low priced vendor. Only 20 guilders as opposed to 25 everywhere else.

Anyway, we ordered a pot of tea, rolled up a doob, and just kinda freaked out at the whole unreal scene. Sitting in a coffee shop and smoking a joint, and it was as natural as could be. Maybe there will be hope for America someday beyond the 23 Legal states, 2 territories, and D.C.?

Nothing was left to chance. They even had your choice of Space Cakes at the register on the way out. Having never tried any "edibles" before, I was intrigued by the Space Cakes. It looked like a little slice of pound cake, but it was baked with a certain amount of hashish in it. We each bought one and left to explore a city built in the 1600s. Almost everything is even older than most of what we saw in London. We headed down the street towards the Rijksmuseum which was located in a big plaza. By the time we got there, that Space Cake had kicked in. I was higher than I think I've ever been before, but it was great.

There were pigeons everywhere! All European cities have an overabundance of pigeons, but this was out of control! There was a little boy who couldn't have been much older than 3 or 4 years. His parents bought him a little bag of bird feed so he could feed the pigeons. Well, the birds had this kid's number. They realized he was a small human, low to the ground, who had food. After they surrounded him on the ground, the birds started landing on him. First his head, then his shoulders. When he became really frightened he put out his arms, and the birds landed on them. This poor kid had pigeons all over him! It was something out of an Alfred Hitchcock movie! Where the hell were this poor kid's parents?!

Amsterdam had a lot of strange leaning buildings. The city was built in the 17th century on land that was retrieved from the North Sea, so their foundations weren't the most stable for the long run. It was interesting to notice that if I were standing on the curb of the street, the top of the building I'm standing in front of might be directly overhead. Not all buildings did that though, some leaned left, right, back, or forward depending on where they were. Nonetheless, this was a very interesting observation, especially when you're high.

The juxtaposition of a sex shop sharing a common wall with a house of worship?? Only in Amsterdam!

I had heard stories about The Leidseplein and the entertainment around that area from friends back home, so we decided to make our way over there. On the way, we stumbled across one of the Great Bastions of Beer – The Original Heineken Brewery that was built sometime back in 1873. Wow! This beat the hell out of another museum day!

The queue was long and filled with American and Canadian college students, but it was worth the wait. The actual tour only took about 20 minutes. This building was the original brewery built in the 19th century, and it was in the midst of brewing its last batches. It was still making beer when we visited, but Heineken was ceasing beer making operations there, and it was going to be only a museum.

After the walking tour, we went into a presentation room with a big projection screen at the head of the room, along with a fresh keg and big platters of meats, cheeses, and crackers. We all sat down and were shown a video of how Heineken is brewed. When the lights went out the doobs sparked up. After all, it was Amsterdam! Heck, Szyd and I didn't even need to pull out our stash. People from every direction were handing us joints. What a party?! The tour group we were with finished off the first keg, so the hospitable Dutch naturally tapped a second keg for us. How could we refuse?

From the top of the old Heineken Brewery built in 1873

We eventually made it to the Leidseplein, an entertainment district of Amsterdam. We were looking for a place called The

50

Bulldog which was highly recommended by a friend back home in Chicago. She said it was better than the Hard Rock Cafe which was also on the Leidseplein. We'd soon learn the differences between coffee shops and bars in this town. It basically breaks down like this. You can't sell weed or hash over the same counter that you sell alcohol over. In other words, you cannot buy it or smoke it at the bar. There was a guy sitting at a dark table in the corner with his bag of wares. You could buy from him and go back to a table away from the bar to have a smoke.

One of the original Hard Rock Cafes

Besides being intoxicated, walking in Amsterdam was an experience. They had the old sidewalks built centuries ago right up along the buildings. They had the streetcar rails in the center of a four lane road, and those and the two outside lanes were for cars. What confused us was what we thought was a wide sidewalk between the street and the old sidewalk so you could all walk abreast of each other. No, it wasn't a walkway at all. It was probably the first designated bicycle lanes I'd ever seen. We almost got run over a few times until we figured out that we were wrong.

Bicycles ruled in Amsterdam. The city was flat, no hills, so riding a bike was easy. It seemed like everybody had one. We noticed that you could easily find a parking spot for your car, but you would have a hard time trying to find a piece of a railing or something to chain your bike to. England had a lot of bicycle riders but not like this.

At night, we had to go see the world infamous Amsterdam Red Light District. This place was like a walk through Playboy magazine! All of the streets were walking only. The neighborhood was so old that no cars or motorized traffic could ever hope to go through.

These businesses were something unlike I'd ever seen before. There was a really small picture window with a door on the side. The girl would pose herself in some erotic fashion to entice potential customers to knock and do business. When one of the crowd of tourists in these alleyways would knock on a door to do business, all the spectators, including us, would gather around to see how a legal prostitution transaction took place. She had a little hostess table with her log books just like a normal business. On the wall over her hostess table were her business licenses and daily health check-up records. Remember, this was 1989. HIV and AIDS were still misunderstood and running rampant. Buyer beware!

The window decor was interesting as well. In America during the Reagan years, we had the "Just Say No!" campaign. That was Nancy Reagan's miserably failed attempt to get kids off drugs. Yeah, right Nancy. That'll work. Anyway, Amsterdam had its own anti-drug campaign. "Say No to Hard Drugs". They posted stickers on the store windows of the prostitutes showing syringes surrounded by a red circle and a line through it with the slogan on it. There were also window stickers showing a camera with a red circle around it and a slash through it, and they were serious about that one!

They had these big goons at either end of these little alleys kind of like bouncers. Well a few of these voyeurs thought they could take a snapshot without the goons seeing them. Too bad these geniuses didn't think about the flash. Instantly, the goons came barreling down the alley from two different directions. One grabbed the guy and another grabbed his camera ripping the film out of the back! This chump not only lost the photo opportunity, but also his whole roll of film.

Because everything on this whole European escapade is so novel, we were learning new things left, right, and center. Public transportation was no exception. In Britain as in America, everyone pays their fare without exception. On the continent, we soon learned paying your fare could be optional. The big streetcars rolled through Amsterdam with big windows so you could see everything, including the conductors coming from a mile away. The driver didn't take your fare. He or she just drove the streetcar. The conductors would get on and off various cars at various stops. Conductors stuck out like sore thumbs in their uniforms, hats, and fare boxes around their necks. You just watched out the window when the streetcar was approaching a stop. If you saw a conductor about to get on the streetcar, you just got off and waited for the next one. You did just the opposite if you were waiting for the streetcar. Look in the window to see if there's a conductor. If so, you waited for the next streetcar. They came by so often that it wasn't a big deal.

I don't really remember getting back to London, and I'm not really surprised. But when we met back up with our classmates who went to Edinburgh and compared notes, the wildest thing they encountered were very forward women who bought drinks for men. Someday Bryan is going to wish he stuck to our original plan.

10 – Classes in the Field

D ay trips were plentiful. We had loads of classes in the field, but the Kents took us on day trips as well to places like Hampton Court and Kew Gardens. Mr. Kent, being a professor of die-casting at Hounslow Community College, was the consummate educator, and he wanted to present his beloved England and the British Empire to everyone who crossed his threshold.

Our big field trip was an overnighter when we went cross country to Swansea, Wales with Dr. Mark Sleep and his British Geology and Scenery class. Of course he had his lovely graduate student working as an assistant on this trip. We arrived at our B&B in the evening so we could get a nice early start on the next day. When coming out of our room in the morning, we witnessed the "professorial walk of shame"! This was classic! The geology guy who taught us about how stalactites come down from the ceiling of a cave because "tights, gentlemen, were meant to come down". I never again forgot the difference between stalactites and stalagmites, nor the irony of seeing himself and his graduate assistant coming out of the same room in the morning.

Dr. Sleep brought us down to the southern coast of Wales where we could observe the chalk cliffs that go down to the sea. It was amazing to think that these things were made out of what the teacher wrote with on the old blackboard back in the day. In order to look over the cliffs, we were strongly advised to lay down on our stomachs first, then slowly crawl toward the edge and look over with only your head. We were told that, all too often, people will look over from a standing position and, for some reason, be drawn forward to fall on the beach below. I was hoping that he didn't know that from first-hand experience, because we were under his watch at the time.

This was the trip where my camera shutter was damaged resulting in 3 rolls of unexposed film when I got back to The States. A good friend, Meghan, was an amateur photographer and studying to do it professionally so she was the obvious choice to ask to take a photo of me doing something stupid like walking out on a chalk bridge to a pillar of chalk about 300 feet above the beach below. It seemed like a good idea at the time. I would find myself saying that all too often on this journey. Anyway, something happened and she dropped my camera on some rocky ground. I couldn't blame her though. It was a pure accident. Cameras were her life, and she wasn't the type to be randomly careless.

Swansea's Chalk Cliffs before the camera drop and after the drop.

This incident is why one should journal when one travels. I'm not talking about some random week during winter when you go somewhere warm like Mexico, but rather when you're going on an excursion for an extended period of time. Even if your camera survives and takes beautiful photos, you'll probably never remember all the details. Journaling brings back all of the memories.

Brighton, on the southern coast of Britain, was another weekend day-trip we took with school. It's only about 47 miles south of London and the closest beachside resort town to the city. Brighton is most well-known for The Royal Pavilion. The palace was built in 1787, and was actively lived in during the Regent era between George III and Victoria. In other words, the 1800s. It was built in an Indian style of architecture which made it unique among other royal residences. Palace Pier or Brighton Pier was another big attraction. It extends some 1700+ feet out into the English Channel and provides a great view of the town. It opened in 1899 and was a popular destination along with the beach among Victorian era Londoners who had easy access via a well-established railway system.

Another weekend, we went to Windsor Castle just west of London. A little beyond the airport literally. It's the oldest occupied castle in the world, built by William the Conqueror in the late 12th century. Because it's occupied, the public can't tour the inside of the castle, so tourists keep themselves busy by touring the grounds and the picturesque town of Windsor. This town is also home to Eaton College where Princes William and Harry would later study. The irony of this day-trip came at a little tourist trinket shop across the street from the castle. I bought a button sized pin that looked like the warning label on a pack of cigarettes. But instead of warning against cigarettes, it said HM (her majesty's) Government can seriously damage your health. Being an Irishman, I wore it proudly.

11 - We Love Live Music

We were in London. The home of such great rock and roll that we couldn't pass up the opportunity to experience what the city had to offer. Like most major cities, London has various newspapers to find music venues. We were always looking to see Eric Clapton at the Hammersmith Odeon, because he seemed to play there often, but that never happened. We did, though, have what seemed to be a brush with fame in that same neck of the woods.

We went to a venue in the Hammersmith neighborhood along the Piccadilly Line on the Underground so it wasn't far from home. We went to see this band that was recommended by some friends. For the life of me, I can't remember the name of the band, but they were great. They were a blues/rock band that liked to get into an occasional jam. I particularly noticed that the bassist looked like John-Paul Jones from Led Zeppelin, and also played a wood-grained Rickenbacher bass guitar with 6 strings.

The "time-bell" eventually rang which signaled last-call in England, so it was time to drink up. We wanted to talk to the band a bit because they were so good, and we went up to the stage as they were packing up their instruments.

We had a bit of banter back and forth, until I asked the bassist, "Hey, has anyone ever told you that you bear a striking resemblance to John Paul-Jones from Led Zeppelin?" They all fell silent and looked at the bassist. He just flashed an embarrassed or coy smile, looked down, and walked away giggling which would follow with what I've read about him. Jones was the shy one of Led Zeppelin. He'd go along the back wall of the hotel lobby while the others would walk right up in front of the cameras. We never had any confirmation, but I think that was my brush with fame!

Ijaz and Riaz were at their music venue search again when they came across one in London's East End. Now, the issue wasn't that it was just far away, the East End was the poorer, dodgy part of town. This is where the famous English Cockneys come from. By this time, Mr. Kent had become alarmed again with some of the neighborhoods in London I've chosen to visit, but Bryan and Szyd were coming with me this time. We weren't afraid of London. The average cop, or Bobbie, doesn't even carry a gun! How dangerous could it be?

It took so long to get there that we missed most of the show. The band seemed to be more of a punk rock band than "progressive rock". That's what the Brits call classic rock, although, I think the name "progressive" is more descriptive of the genre, e.g. Led Zeppelin, Deep Purple, Cream, or just a guitar with an "edge".

The neighborhood was as dodgy as hell. Public housing projects everywhere instead of the average row-houses of England. There was also shit for street lighting or any other kind of illumination. It was a ripe scenario for Jack the Ripper.

We grabbed a few cans of beer at the Off License (Liquor/beer store) for the long trip back to Isleworth. The Tube only took us as far as the city center though, and then it stopped running for the night. In order to get home, Ijaz and Riaz led us to Trafalgar Square to catch the midnight bus. There, there were late night buses that spiral outward into London's night in a spider fashion going out in all directions.

We got on the bus after Ijaz had a brief altercation with the bus driver. I was just walking up to the bus door when I saw him insisting quite vehemently that the driver was "out of line". Anyway, we went up to the second floor of the bus where some of the guys could have a cigarette. No smoking on the first floor of the bus. Afterall, it was a long trip from Trafalgar Square to the Osterley stop on the Piccadilly Line, much less taking a bus through the winding streets of London.

So, we cracked a beer and some of the boys lit up a cigarette for the long bus ride home. We were all in a social mood, and there were some other guys upstairs on the bus who also had a beer and a cigarette. We all introduced ourselves to each other and started "shooting the shit". Somehow, they and I figured out we had Irish-born parents. They were Irish-Englishmen just like I'm an Irish-American, and we all grew up culturally Irish!

Woo-Hoo!! An Irish sing-a-long soon began. It was a long road home, and we sang all kinds of Irish songs. We even sang IRISH REBEL SONGS on the midnight bus driving through London. Ijaz was floored! He knew my parents were from Ireland, but he didn't know I was THAT Irish.

My "sainted" grandmother (mom's mother), who was decorated for bravery in the Women's Auxiliary during Ireland's fight for freedom from the British, would have been proud! Erin Go Bragh! Up the Rebels! As they'd say in Ireland!

Much later, I visited the Glastonbury Rock Festival. It's the granddaddy of all British rock festivals. It was modeled after Woodstock, but the big difference is that Glastonbury has been going on annually since 1970. Our friends Ijaz and Riaz had been telling us about Glastonbury since we first met. It was the high-point of the music festival season and a definite must-see. Unfortunately for my roommates Szyd and Bryan, Glastonbury was held in the middle of summer and they would be back in America by that time. On the other hand, I was going to stay and work in England during the summer, so I'd be there for the concert.

It took place on a farmer's personal field out in southwestern England. Somerset, to be exact. This was the part of England that the fabled King Arthur ruled over. According to Ijaz, the valley that the main stage was built in was a retrieved swamp. Centuries ago, there used to be a lake there, and that's where "The Lady of the Lake" appeared to Arthur with the sword Excalibur. That was more than enough to make the freaky people come out of the woodwork.

Well, it was summer and I was working as a carpenter on a new industrial park in Harlow, a northeastern suburb of London outside of the M25 Orbital Motorway. They have long weekends from time to time in Britain that they call "Bank Holidays". I guess if there's no real holiday in a given month, they just make one up. Not a bad idea.

So, I packed a small bag and made my way down to Victoria Station where many an excursion started. You could tell right away that almost everyone at the bus depot area of Victoria Station was heading for the concert. Glastonbury is pretty much straight west of London along the M4 Motorway (Interstate). The bus driver was observant. Although the sign on the front of the bus said Glastonbury, that town is actually 6 miles from the concert itself. He sent a poll around to the passengers, and the result was that he'd just drive us straight to the front entrance of the show. BONUS!!

I did have the money to pay for a ticket the honest way, but in following the tradition of "scamming our way across Europe", I wanted to see if there was an alternative way into the show. I took a walk around the perimeter of the place to see if there were any "weak spots" in their barriers. There wasn't much to find. They had 10 foot tall sheet metal panels all assembled one next to the other. Climbing it was out of the question, and I couldn't jump high enough to grab the top. There were also helicopters in the air looking for people just like me. As I walked along the road, the wall took a turn away from it. Under a tree and off to the side, I noticed, out of freaking nowhere, a long section of pipe that was bent in the middle and had a flange (square metal piece) welded to the end. Well, I turned into MacGyver and made something out of nothing.

I took that pipe with the flange and wedged the flange between two of the metal panels of the wall. Then, I just walked up the bent part until I could grab the top of the wall. I hopped over the wall and did it all under a tree and out of view of the helicopters. But I wasn't out of danger. Other music fans that wanted to sneak their way in saw what I was doing. I heard them hollering things like, "Look at that bloke over there! He found a way in!". Once I landed on the other side of the wall, I took off running. When I looked back I saw others following my lead and the helicopters coming back at the same time. All I knew was that I made it in and saved £28 by figuring out a way to scale a wall. Cheers to MacGyver!

The headliners in 1989 were Elvis Costello, Van Morrison, and Suzanne Vega. Rumors were running around that the Grateful Dead were going to play which is why I was so adamant on going, but that never came to fruition. Bummer! That would have been great!

While I was exploring the place on my own, I was keeping my eyes open for my English classmates Ijaz and Riaz. They were at home in Southampton for the summer, so we just planned on meeting there, which was an almost improbable proposition.

That night, I shivered my ass off! The summer of 1989 in England was the driest, warmest summer they had had in decades, but at night it still cooled off incredibly. I was trying to sleep secludedly on my own at first, but then I got chilly enough to where I introduced myself to some people with a little fire and asked if I could curl up next to it and share the warmth. I got lucky, I was among hippie-types. They were into sharing.

The next morning was an experience in hippie fashion and hygiene. Many more people had arrived at the show, and the farmer had water spigots set up in various places on the grounds so people could wash up, drink water, etc. British hippies dress very differently than American ones. I had been to enough Grateful Dead shows back home to know. Instead of tie-dye clothes and thread-bare cut-off blue jeans, British hippies dressed Medieval. It looked kind of like a renaissance fair. All except for this one guy waiting in the queue for water to wash up. He was wearing nothing but a pair of shoes with a towel draped over his arm like a butler and a bar of soap in his hand. In his defense though, he wasn't bothering anybody and nobody was bothering him, although he did seem rather friendly and social as if nothing was amiss. Maybe it's good to be secure in your own body image?

I noticed some vendors with tables set up selling their wares. One of them was selling old blankets for only £1! Wow, I didn't care where it came from or how it looked. I wasn't going to shiver that night.

I spent most of the day just walking around and taking in the whole scene. Always keeping an eye out for my classmates, Ijaz and Riaz. In reality, the odds of meeting up with them were astronomical. We didn't have cellular phones, the internet, or any kind of other technology to help us connect. We just said that we'd meet somewhere on the left side of the main stage. Well, lo and behold! Just walking along, I almost tripped over them. They had their blanket spread out and set up a "camp". This was most welcomed because I was really tired of wandering around. Besides, going to a rock festival is always fun, but not as much when you're on your own.

This party was about to take a turn into the world of Lewis Carroll and Alice in Wonderland. Great English literature! We weren't going down rabbit holes though, and it sure as hell wasn't the Disney version. It's well known that Lewis Carroll chowed down on psilocybin mushrooms when he wrote "Alice". That's where he came up with so much of his imagery.

We call them either Magic Mushrooms or just Shrooms in the States, but they look very different in Britain. In America, you get big "caps and stems" with your shrooms. In Britain you got a whole bunch of little, tiny mushrooms that looked like bean sprouts, or tadpoles. Little heads with a long skinny tail, and instead of eating just a few, I was instructed to chow about 30 of them. That was it and the show was on! My biggest memory was when Suzanne Vega played after nightfall, which was really late in England in June. A fog started rolling into the valley the main stage was in. When the light show kicked in with the fog, it made for great "visuals"! Even simple spotlights were making what appeared to be huge lighted tubes through the fog. It was an amazing spectacle. The fog just added to the mystical type scene there in the land of Avalon.

The way home on Sunday was another odyssey back to London. It started out well because the motorcoaches just showed up at the concert venue instead of us having to find our way to the town of Glastonbury six miles away. But our good fortune didn't last long. On the way back, our bus broke down on the side of the M4 Motorway. After a while, some genius decided that they needed to send a new bus to us so we could get home in a reasonable amount of time. This took four hours. In the meantime, I got to know some of my fellow travelers. I had a little hash stash but no way to smoke it, and they had some tobacco and rolling papers. We joined efforts and enjoyed some British joints. The British don't smoke buds like Americans do, and you can't roll a joint out of hashish chunks. Since pre-rolled cigarettes were expensive in Britain, many people rolled their own tobacco. Well what hash smokers did was to heat up the edge of a chunk of hash, then flake the hash into the tobacco, roll it up, and smoke away.

I used to be a cigarette smoker, but I was off of them for two and a half years at that time. Smoking this way eventually got me back to smoking cigarettes again. Big mistake!

So the second bus arrived to save us, and the drivers had to transfer all of our bags over to our new ride. We finally got going and arrived back at Victoria Station in central London, and I needed to get back to Southgate on the Underground. It was very late by the time I arrived at Breege and Steve's house, and they were convinced I was in jail when I walked in the door. Ironically, they were listening to some Eric Clapton when the song "If I Don't Be There By Morning" came on. This song has a line that says, "If I don't be there by morning, I must have spent the night in jail." They declared it as my new theme song.

12 - PARIS, FRANCE
Friday 3/17/1989 – Oh shit!

Our semester carried on in a normal way except we were on the other side of the ocean. As mentioned earlier, our Study-Tour started on St. Patrick's Day, but I couldn't NOT celebrate with my cousins up in Southgate, London. I would just meet everyone down at Victoria Station in the morning. No worries...

Of course, I woke up late at my cousin's flat and ran down to the Southgate Tube stop where I took the Piccadilly Line to Green Park and connected to the Victoria Line down to Victoria Station as fast as I possibly could. I missed the damned train to Paris by 10 minutes! You could almost set your watch by Western European trains! I hated it at the moment, but I'd grow to appreciate on-time trains.

My instinct told me to phone Mrs. Kent to see if she knew anything. Thank God, Bryan and Szyd left a message with her that they were going to Gare du Nord in Paris, and the hotel was called Hotel du Nord. Great, what or where the hell were those? Now, I had to pay out of pocket to get to the continent which would prove to be an all too real foreshadowing in getting off of it. The information from Mrs. Kent felt kind of slim at the time, but it's all I had to go on, so Paris, here I come.

My biggest challenge was that I felt like I was coming down with a cold. It wasn't just a hangover from our pre-St. Patrick's Day celebration though. I felt kind of warm, I wasn't nauseous, and it hurt when I looked out of the corner of my eyes. When you're feeling like this, you're obviously not at the top of your game. I had to change money on the ferry to French francs and got about 6 francs to a dollar. On the train from Calais to Paris, I bought a Coke from the snack-guy. He must have known that I was half asleep and feeling like shit, because he took advantage of me in classic French style. He charged me 45 francs or just over $7 for a freaking Coke! I felt so horrible, I didn't even realize it until it was too late.

Gare du Nord, Paris, France

I finally arrived in Paris at Gare du Nord, one of the busiest train stations in northern Europe, feeling like "death warmed over". Now, I had to find Hotel du Nord somewhere in this huge city. Luck works in strange ways, because when I walked out of the train station, I looked up and the big, illuminated sign said Hotel du Nord. Yahoo, I've arrived!

Needless to say, I was rather upset with Dr. O'Neill for leaving me behind in London, and suffering from a cold wasn't helping my disposition. After I checked in, I stormed up this spiral staircase to find Dr. O'Neill and give him a piece of my mind. I was furious and didn't have a really good filter on my mouth at 21 years old, so I think the whole hotel heard my displeasure. I warned him that if he ever left another student behind without a plan, he'd have me to answer for it. Most of the rest of my classmates were NOT seasoned travelers like I was and might not have made it through the obstacles I did to get to Paris on my own.

Anyway, I found my room with Bryan and Szyd, of course, and got settled in for a few days in Paris. It was St. Patrick's Day in Paris, and I was feeling sick as a dog. There wasn't a beer to be found, so I drank a little wine. That didn't last long, so I just went to bed early.

In our room, we had a queen size bed and a twin. Szyd and I shared the queen bed and Bryan was supposed to take the twin. I went to bed early, so I didn't know anything until I awoke in the middle of the night. Szyd was sleeping next to me, and he was also awake. We heard loud snoring from across the room. Szyd shared a bedroom at the Kent's house with Bryan, and said Bryan didn't snore. We could also tell by the light from the street coming in the window, it was not Bryan. So, who was this?

We got up and snuck over to the other bed to see who the hell was there? Lo and behold, it was Kim! What the hell was she doing there? Anyway, we just let her sleep and walked away. In the morning, we had a good laugh.

As it worked out, Bryan and Cheryl had been having a relationship since London. They apparently wanted to celebrate their first night in Paris, the City of Love. Kim was Cheryl's roommate, so Kim and Bryan decided to swap rooms to achieve their ends. Kim had Bryan's key, so she never woke up Szyd and me.

Saturday 3/18/1989 – The Louvre was Closed

We got up at 7:30 am so we could leave at 9am, and we got introduced to the famed Paris Metro. The Metro didn't have anything on London's Underground. It really smelled like a combination of urine and wine puke. But its redeeming quality is that it was really quiet compared to other subway systems because it ran on Michelins instead of iron wheels.

Bryce Vetter, Dr. O'Neill's graduate assistant, took us for a long walk along the Seine River today. The only problem is that we just had to walk past the Louvre. It was closed for renovations. No seeing the Mona Lisa for us. We then walked back to Notre Dame where Dr. O'Neill gave us his own personal tour of the cathedral.

Notre Dame Cathedral's façade, and a ¾ view with classmates

71

Notre Dame is extremely impressive. Its Gothic architecture with the flying buttresses, gargoyles, and intricate decorations is absolutely amazing. When the cathedral was built sometime around the 12th or 13th centuries, everyone was pretty much illiterate. To overcome this challenge, the architects would portray biblical stories in the decorative stonework and stained glass, and the uneducated masses could then understand the stories of the bible. Kind of like years ago in America when they made "the classics" that you read in high school into comic books. It's the same concept.

Afterwards, we walked back up the Seine past The National Assembly Building. This was the French version of Capitol Hill. The guards there were rather intimidating though. They all had automatic weapons which seemed a little less decorative and more pragmatic, like they were expecting something?

We continued along The Seine to The Eiffel Tower and took a small detour so we could walk through the park and take some classic photos. We would have gone up in the tower, but the queue that day was hundreds of people deep, and we were hungry anyhow.

Most continental shops and restaurants post their menus in the window so you can overlook the "board of fare" before going in, and we found a French Delicatessen with an appealing menu. There were nine or ten of us, and I went in first to order. I was well traveled before this semester, but France was the first foreign speaking country I'd ever been to. I thought I'd do the respectful thing and at least attempt to speak their language. WRONG!! When I made an honest attempt to speak HIS language, this cocky Frog looked at me with an attitude and said, "I can speak English, you know!"

Of course, I took offense and told him, in no uncertain terms, I'd take my business elsewhere because of his rudeness. He said to me that one American's business made no difference to him... until I told him that the other nine people reading his menu in the window were with me, and we were ALL going. Just then, he drastically changed his tone, "Ah but monsieur, maybe we can make a deal?" I told him to fuck off! This guy would set the tone for the general feel we'd receive from Parisians in general. They're very rude people, but we found it's not just Americans they dislike. They hate other Frenchmen too just because they're not Parisians.

After we eventually found something to eat, we played some more hacky sack in the park behind Notre Dame Cathedral for about an hour. We found it was actually a good way to loosen up your leg muscles after so much walking. The Europeans, in general, seemed to take an interest in it, probably because of the foot-to-eye coordination kind of like soccer.

That night we stopped at the grocery store for dinner and picked up some items that didn't need refrigeration.

Sunday 3/19/1989 – Palm Sunday

This morning we went back to Notre Dame Cathedral, but this time it was for Palm Sunday Mass. It was an incredible experience being there. They still light the place with candelabras. It was difficult to follow the mass because it was in French, but I was an altar-boy so I could figure out where we were. Also, if I don't know the story of The Passion by now, it's time to go back to religion class. Even though the church was packed, we somehow managed to get seats, which was a blessing. The Passion is just as long in French as it is in English.

After mass, we walked down to the D'Orsay Museum. It had a collection of French paintings, sculptures, and examples of architecture. By this time, we had seen an untold number of museums. We were kind of getting a little museum-ed out, which is probably why none of us were terribly enthused about the D'Orsay. That and we had to skip the granddaddy of all art museums, The Louvre. I was pissed about that.

The Basilica of Sacre Coeur

Sacre Coeur Basilica was our next stop. It was a beautiful church which was way up on a hill. Probably, the only hill I saw in Paris? Therefore, the view was impeccable. You could see the whole city of Paris from up there. Its design wasn't Gothic like so many older churches in Europe, but rather it's more of a Byzantine style that was built in 1875.

It was a beautiful place where a lot of college students hung out, so we figured we would too and find out if something was supposed to happen? In other words, what's everyone looking at? We figured pictures would last longer, so we took some snapshots and skedaddled.

We heard rumors of a pub that sold beers for 6 francs ($1). It was like looking for the rumored Shangri-La, and when we finally found it, it was closed. Figures. So, we went back to our hotel all dejected and jonesing for some good beer. The famed City of Lights didn't seem to have much in the way of nightlife?

That is until we met our night time Front Desk guy at Hotel du Nord. It turns out that he was an expatriate from Chicagoland and went to Loyola Academy High School. He was a pretty cool guy and recommended a pub called Le Violon Dingue on St. Genevieve Street. We'd all meet there that evening, but we arrived at different times. Happy Hour was from 6-9pm, and we wanted to be punctual. In our rushing, we somehow got lost in the winding streets of what I thought was the perpetually trendy Left Bank near the Sorbonne, otherwise known as the University of Paris.

Well the great navigators, Bryan, Szyd, and myself were lost until we heard someone speaking English. We thought oh, thank God! Two men just finished their conversation, so we walked up to the remaining guy and asked him if he could help us because we were lost and heard him speaking English. He asked if we were Americans, and of course we replied Yes. Then we encountered the RUDEST Parisian of them all! He said NO just because we were Americans, even though he spoke perfect English. Well this incensed Szyd to no end! Szyd's a big guy, but he's a gentle giant and mild mannered being very respectful of others…until now. Szyd, out of nowhere, pushed Bryan and me aside to get right in this Frog's face, then hollered, "Oh yeah?! Well, fuck you Frog! Because if it wasn't for us, you'd be speaking fucking German!" Holy shit! Bryan and I were falling over laughing our asses off! Meanwhile, I think I saw steam coming out of the Frenchman's ears!

We eventually found our way to the pub which would be revisited numerous times while in Paris. Le Violon Dingue was co-owned by a British guy and a Minnesotan, so we just knew we found our Parisian hang-out.

Our crowd all left at different times, and Bryan, Szyd and I left kinda late. On the Metro during late night, the characters really come out of the woodwork. There were these guys who had what had to be wigs? I couldn't imagine they could actually grow some big, permed Louis XVI style mullet, but there it was. What was even funnier was that they thought they were bad-asses. They actually wanted to brawl in the Metro for no apparent reason other than we're Americans. Well, we had had a few pints and we were almost happy to oblige, until they found out we were from Chicago. Then out of nowhere, the big haired leader of this group wasn't such a bad-ass anymore. They got off at the next stop, and all tension was diffused.

Monday 3/20/1989 – Chartres

Built in the 12th century, Chartres marked the high point of French Gothic Architecture.

Today was our day trip to Chartres, one of the biggest and most beautiful of Europe's Gothic cathedrals. The day's weather started out great, but later, it turned cold and rainy. Poor Szyd only wore a sweatshirt and froze later in the day. I could appreciate his misery after having had to hike home from Heathrow to the Kent's house back in London in the February rain.

Chartres was probably the most stunning and impressive of the cathedrals we've seen so far. Inside, like most European Catholic cathedrals, they had relics stored. Relics are items associated with a saint, martyr or other sacred person, preserved as worthy of veneration. The most famous relic they have stored there was a dress that The Virgin Mary supposedly wore when she gave birth to Jesus.

The stained glass windows are also one of Chartres' most famous features. One of the colors used in the windows is designated as "Chartres Blue". We were told that that particular shade of blue wasn't even duplicatable in 1989. Who knows if they can do it as of this writing, but that's an astonishing medieval feat of coloring.

Before the rain started, Szyd, Bryan, Chris, and I played hacky sack again in a park behind the cathedral. My hacky sack has come to be an invaluable little time killer. Whenever we have to sit around and wait for whatever it may be, we pull out the hack, form a circle, and kick it around, usually attracting some observers to play regardless of what language they spoke. Hacky sack diplomacy!

After dinner, we all met up at Le Violon Dingue again, only this time, we didn't have to ask for directions on the way.

Tuesday 3/21/1989 – Champs de Elysee

We met Dr. O'Neill at Invalides this morning. Invalides was a hospital built by Louis XIV for the wounded soldiers. In the chapel was where Napoleon's tomb was located. Not being too interested in Napoleon's grave, we walked down to the Place de Concorde which is a famous busy roundabout in Paris. Right in the middle of the roundabout is a huge obelisk named Cleopatra's Needle. Of course, Napoleon brought it to Paris after looting as much treasure as they could from Egypt after his men blew the nose off the Sphinx.

Nearby the Place de Concorde, we saw an impressive building called The Church of the Madeleine. You'd never know it was a church, though. It's a neoclassical building that looks like something right out of either Greece or Rome.

We broke with the pack from there and went to check out the Champs de Elysee. That's like the "Paris Strip" with all kinds of super-luxury apartments and high-end retail shops. It's connected on either end by the Place de Concorde and the Arc de Triomphe. It's a famous view from one end to the other. Along the way, we came across stores that were so fancy, ritzy, and up-scale that it would almost be too expensive to window shop. McDonald's even fell into that category so we just had to go in to see how the other half ate malnutrition on a bun. The menu was interesting because the metric system was first invented in France. Because of that, they didn't have a Quarter Pounder with Cheese listed on the menu because they would know what the hell a quarter pound was. They called it a Royale with Cheese instead. I think what made this McDonald's so upscale is that they sold BEER! Well, we had to buy a beer just to be able to say we bought a beer in McDonald's. It was pure crap, but we did it.

Our next stop was the Arc de Triomphe at the far end of the Champs de Elysee. It's a roundabout with the Arc in the middle of it and 6 major streets spiraling off in different directions. The circular lanes around it are crazy too. There's six lanes going around if I remember correctly. Thank God there's an underground walkway so you can get out to the Arc. It was beginning to rain so we went back to the hotel and hung out for a while.

Even with all of our travels around Paris, we couldn't find a single other pub that specialized in beer, so we went back to Le Violon Dingue. These guys are getting to know us.

Wednesday 3/22/1989 – Versailles

Today was our day-trip to Versailles just outside of town. The palace was as incredible as the history books made it out to be. It was designed to host 3000 of Louis XIV's closest Royals and Noble friends. Could you imagine what a wretched nest of deceit, scum and villainy that must have been?

Versailles Palace

We couldn't get into the palace until 2:30 pm, so we went into the gardens out in the back and had some lunch. Szyd didn't bring anything in his bag to eat, so he just mooched off of everyone else. Oh well, it happens, and it's not like they have food vendors on the grounds of Versailles Palace which are stunning, by the way. Mel Brooks in the movie History of the World Part I didn't do justice to the intricate grooming they have going on here. So with time to kill once again, we pulled out the hacky sack amidst all of this gardening glory and played until we could go into the palace to see the insides.

The inside was even more impressive than the outside. Every room was highly and ornately decorated. They also had paintings on every ceiling in every room. Then there's the Hall of Mirrors. I would have loved to have been the Windex salesman who had that account! Everyone (for the most part) has seen the Hall of Mirrors. It was the famous room in which The Treaty of Versailles was signed ending World War I. There's a photo of it in every history textbook in America, albeit in black and white, so the resolution wasn't that good.

The Gardens at Versailles – "It's good to be the King" – Mel Brooks

When we got back, Szyd found some beer we could take back to the hotel, because we had some planning to do. Seven of us were going to go to Greece at the end of the semester, which was 4/2/1989, and time was closing in fast. Kim and I had a friend we knew in Chicago named Christos who was a native of Corinth, Greece. Chris, Kim, and I planned back in Chicago during the fall semester to meet in Greece, because he was going to be home at the time Kim and I would be in Europe. It wasn't really smart to travel alone in Europe, unless you're very streetwise, and know how to defend yourself. So, we didn't do that. I was traveling with Bryan and Szyd, and Kim was traveling with Cheryl, Kelly, and Karen. Now, it wasn't just two of us showing up at Chris' house, there were seven of us! We didn't even realize yet what an adventure we were in for.

Thursday 3/23/1989 – Last Day in Paris

This was the morning we packed up our stuff and headed to Gare de Lyon train station where we locked up our bags in lockers in preparation for our journey to Rome that evening. Every train station conveniently had various sized coin operated lockers where you could store your bags while touring. These would come in immensely valuable along our travels.

The 100ᵗʰ Anniversary of the Eiffel Tower and the view from second level

From there, Szyd, Bryan and I walked over to the Eiffel Tower to see if we could accomplish what we couldn't last Saturday. The line for tickets wasn't as bad as it was before. Probably because it was a weekday out of tourist season. Anyway, we walked up to the second level. It was a long way up, but the view was great. Paris had an ordinance in the city that no building could be taller than six stories, so we could see everything just like at Sacre Coeur. There really wasn't a reason to spend the big francs just to get to the top to see what we already could see.

Still killing time for the most part, we learned of a cemetery nearby that contained the grave of Jim Morrison, the lead singer of the late 60s band The Doors. At the time of his death in 1971 at age 27, he was an ex-patriate on the run from the law in the US. The American "establishment" back then didn't care for any rock n rollers. Each of us having a bottle of beer left after lunch, we decided we'd go and have a beer and a salute to Jim

Morrison. Unfortunately, the cemetery was horribly defaced with graffiti everywhere. Jim here. Jim there. Jim with arrows pointing to where his grave was. It was very disgraceful and rather disappointing. When we found his grave, the headstone was moved off-center, diagonal and covered in graffiti. There was also a security guard there making sure no one else defaces it any further. Very disappointing.

Jim Morrison's grave as it looked in March 1989

This cemetery was filled with all kinds of famous and infamous people right in the center of Paris. There were so many that they handed out a map of the cemetery with burial plots of the famous people marked throughout. We had to lose the security guard if we were going to have our ceremonial beer. Public drinking in Britain was okay, but we didn't know the laws in Paris? We then came across the grave of Auguste Comte, the father of modern sociology. He must have been a "social guy", so we lifted our last beers to him.

Later, we grabbed the Metro over to St. Michel and walked to Le Violon Dingue so we could be there when happy hour started. Afterall, we had an overnight train to Milan, and a good buzz would help for sleeping on a moving train. But this time we'd have sleeping berths making it easy. All of our subsequent overnight trains wouldn't have near the accommodations.

13 - ROME, ITALY

The train pulled into Milan during the late morning, and we had a three hour layover until our next train to Rome. So, Bryan, Szyd, Chris, Mary, and I went for a walk to find some food and exchange money. Changing money is going to become a major hassle and a pitfall for many travelers. The Euro Standard was one of the best things Europe has done since then.

We weren't 20 yards outside the train station and we were introduced to Italy's gypsies. Two little kids tried to pick Szyd's pocket, but he didn't have anything in it. Then, two other gypsy kids came up to me holding a newspaper flat in her hand and walked up to me. I thought at first that she was some poor child looking to sell a newspaper. Just then, I realized this little street urchin, under the newspaper, had the zipper on my hip-sack halfway open. That was too close for comfort, and we had a whole new perspective on being careful and aware.

We eventually found a bank to change money and then went to Wendy's of all places. Familiar restaurants aren't always the same when you're overseas. It was nothing to write home about.

Eventually, we caught our train to Rome and had a great opportunity to see the Italian landscape. Italy is a really long country. The train ride was long, but we eventually made it to the Roma Termini or their main train station. Our hotel was only a short walk from the station. We washed up and then went looking for a pizzeria that was listed in our travel bible, Let's Go Europe. We ended up at a different pizza joint though, but wow, was it ever good! Italy was going to be a gastronomic experience for us!

Saturday 3/25/1989

This morning, we headed out with Bryce Vetter about 9am. Just wandering around Rome is amazing. We've all seen the photos of Rome from TV, magazines, and the like. Not to mention all of the history books, but being there is beyond words, especially for someone with a keen sense of history.

The Monument to Victor Emmanuel who united the Italian States

We first came to the monument dedicated to Victor Emmanuel, the guy who unified the independent Italian states in 1870. It is also the Italian Tomb of the Unknown Soldier. We then walked over to the Roman Forum which is where the Roman Senate used to gather. Unfortunately, there isn't much left except for the large arch and some columns.

The Colosseum was the next stop on our tour. I know we throw around the word "amazing and incredible" a lot, but the Colosseum really is. The engineering and technology that went into this place spared no expense. They not only held the gladiator games there that we all know about, but also they were able to hold naval battles by diverting the Tiber river to flood the colosseum. That's something modern stadiums cannot do.

The Famous Colosseum outside of which we dined

After the morning session, Bryan, Cheryl, Kelly, Szyd, and I bought some rolls and cheese. Food that doesn't need refrigeration so we could carry it around with us. The perfect place for lunch was this park just across the street from The Colosseum. Sitting there eating our lunch, you just couldn't help looking at that structure in awe. They even had numbered gate entrances which would be numbered on your ticket so you could find your seat easily just like they do today. Of course, a venue as stunning as this required some hacky-sack to aid in digestion.

We walked down by the Tiber River and sat under a bridge on an island. Some of us needed to move into the shade because we were starting to get some color. The weather here is great too. This was the warmest day we've felt since early last fall. It must have been about 75 degrees with no clouds. Yes, we can handle this.

Right nearby, we found by accident The Circus Maximus. This was the big venue for the ancient chariot races. It was huge just like an ancient horse track with tight turns at either end. If I remember correctly, it was also the venue for the movie from Hollywood's gilded age, Ben Hur starring Charlton Heston.

Later, we ate dinner at a little family owned restaurant, then again, they all seemed to be family owned? The food was exquisite. And, what a deal?! We paid about $7 US each for a three course meal and the house wine. Eating good in the neighborhood.

Somehow, somebody found an Irish Pub in the middle of Rome, so after dinner, everyone congregated at a place called The Fiddler's Elbow. It was great! It was down the street from The Termini train station just past a Basilica. Nice and close to our hotel too. We met some guys from Egypt who were very friendly. One of them spoke English and was an interesting guy. The other couldn't speak any English but kept lifting his pint and saying "Condor!" every time he would roll up a cigarette for himself or someone else with Condor Brand tobacco. He was so proud of his one and only English vocabulary word, but he was a nice guy.

Easter Sunday 3/26/1989

Everyone got up early this morning in order to get to Easter Mass at the Vatican celebrated by Pope John Paul II. Trying to get there was a chore. Outside of The Termini train station, there was a sea of people trying to get on a whole load of buses, all of which were going to The Vatican for mass.

While waiting to get on a bus, we witnessed the little gypsy street urchins in action. They were just like the ones we encountered in Milan, only better. One man was plain old victimized when one of the punks got his wallet. But instead of just running, they'd hand it off from one kid to another, and soon the wallet was history in a huge crowd of people. There was also a Japanese man who had a gypsy kid reach in his jacket pocket and grab his wallet. I don't know what he was doing with his wallet in his jacket pocket, but luckily for him, he was lightning quick. He swung his arm out, grabbed her wrist, pulled her in, and kicked her hard in the crotch lifting her off the ground. Her knees buckled, she dropped the wallet, and the whole crowd started applauding and cheering for the little Japanese guy. Wow, our day was off to a flying start!

Public transportation in most of Europe is very efficient, but it's kind of a joke in the way that people pay their fares. Dr. O'Neill taught us that in most European countries, public transportation is subsidized by the government to one degree or another. The percentage that it is subsidized is equal to the same percentage of people who DO NOT pay their bus/train fare. In Italy, that number was 80%! In other words, 80% of Italians don't even pay bus/train fare unless they're forced to by the conductor.

Well, if 80% of Italians aren't paying their bus fare, I'd be damned if I was going to pay. The conductor collected your fare, not the bus driver, and we quickly learned how to avoid paying our fare. Conductors stuck out like sore thumbs in their uniforms, hats, and fare boxes around their necks. You just watched out the window when the bus was approaching a stop. If you saw a conductor about to get on the bus, you just got off and waited for the next one. You did just the opposite if you were waiting for the bus. Look in the bus window to see if there's a conductor. If so, you waited for the next bus. They came by so often that it wasn't a big deal.

It was this day that Szyd, Bryan and I joked about someday writing a book to compete with "Let's Go Europe", our travel bible. We were going to call it "Scamming Your Way Through Europe".

Anyway, we arrived at The Vatican at about 9:45 am, 45 minutes before mass began. As a result, we had a relatively close-up view of the Pope. We were about halfway between the big obelisk in the center of St. Peter's Square and the Basilica itself. It was the perfect spot for some choice photos, and we took advantage of it. Chris is a tall guy, and I'm not. So, I asked him if I could get on his shoulders and take a photo with his camera and one with mine? He said of course, it would be an historic snapshot. So, he squatted, I climbed on his shoulders, and I clicked away. Well, everyone around noticed me on Chris' shoulders and started handing me cameras from every direction in at least six different languages. I must have been up there a long time because poor Chris was getting really tired. He had to let me down.

Easter Sunday on Chris' shoulders at the Vatican with St. John Paul II

By 10:30 am, St. Peter's Square was absolutely packed! A solid crowd of people all the way down the street that leads up to it as well. It almost seemed like a bit of a Pep Rally. There were, understandably, people from everywhere around the world in attendance, but so many made huge banners held up on poles in all kinds of languages. It made for a big spectacle.

After mass, Bryan, Cheryl, Kelly, Szyd, and I went for a walk past The Pantheon and through a bunch of old Roman streets. Like I said before, just walking through Rome is an adventure around every corner. Modern Rome is also nice too. We saw in Pantheon Square a beautiful red Ferrari Turbo GTS. The best of old and new.

When in Rome, do as the Romans do.

We figured when in Rome, do as the Romans do. So, we all decided to have a Roman Toga Party back at our hotel. When we got back, Szyd, Bryan, Chris, and I started setting up for the party. We took the sheets off the beds to use as togas. We even broke off olive branches and made head-wreaths out of them. The event of the night though was when we needed to go on a booze run. As we went through the hotel lobby wearing our togas, the night desk lady almost had a conniption, because she thought we were stealing her sheets. At least that's what it sounded like when she was hollering between Italian and English. We also had fun with the looks we got from people at the liquor store while in our togas.

Monday 3/27/1989

After a tough awakening from the night before, the gang set out for the beach. Our destination was a place called Lido di Ostia which is just a few miles outside Rome on the Tyrannian Sea coast which is a branch of the Mediterranean Sea surrounded by the Italian mainland, Sicily to the south, and Sardinia on the east. I've seen blonde sand and white sand beaches before but for the first time I saw black volcanic sand. It was really weird.

Well, the seven of us, Bryan, Szyd, Chris, Cheryl, Kelly, Mary and I caught some rays on the beach, and of course, we played hacky sack too. Szyd and I walked up the beach both directions from where we were camped out and did a little sightseeing. Most European beaches are topless, and this one was no exception. Mind you, all women can go topless, but not all women should. Some were hot, and some were not. Then there were some that combined both categories. Example: there was this very sexy girl, tan, with long dark hair, and a string bikini laying down leaning back on her elbows. The only problem was the bush of hair growing out of her armpit. It was bigger than mine! Whoa?! Big turn-off!

After the beach, we headed back to the hotel and rested a while before dinner. We had a nice dinner that night compliments of the president's office of Our College, so we dined well. Before food-coma set in, we just hung around the hotel and crashed out later in anticipation of more touring around Rome.

Tuesday 3/28/1989

This morning, a group of us went with Bryce Vetter to see The Vatican Museum which is on the far side of The Vatican from where we entered. The entry fee was $2 cheaper for students than for others, but Szyd forgot his student ID at the hotel. I don't remember how we passed it off, but somehow I slipped my ID to Szyd and it worked.

The museum was very different from what we had been used to. The Sistine Chapel was very busy with a lot of people and kind of rushed. It didn't help that it was covered with scaffolding for cleaning. I'm beginning to think nearly everything in Europe is covered in scaffolding for cleaning. I guess the pollution from The Industrial Revolution really did a number on these antiquities. Much of the art in the museum was fairly dark and gory. You had your spikes in heads, decapitated bodies, and swords in bellies. If art is a reflection of the times in which it was created, I guess this artwork must have been created in very turbulent and much tougher times.

We walked around Vatican City for a little while, and thought I noticed that we were being followed or targeted by some gypsies. Is there no shame? This was The Vatican for God's Sake…no pun intended. We walked out into St. Peter's Square, and they were still there following us. We decided to sit down along the colonnade and eat some food from our bags. The gypsies sat down too just across from us. Once I pulled out my switchblade that I bought in Italy and flicked it open to cut my bread, the gypsies got up and left.

The view from atop of St. Peter's Basilica

St. Peter's Basilica is a fabulous piece of architecture. It's one of the tallest buildings in the surrounding area, so you can see for miles when you climb up to the top of the dome. Down inside the Basilica is an enormous altar structure, and below that is the grave of St. Peter as well as the graves of many popes in the catacombs. There is also no shortage of enormous statues and beautiful chapels. It's a definite must see for the Roman tourist regardless of your faith.

After The Vatican, Bryan wanted to go see the Pantheon and Trevi Fountain. It's almost like EVERYTHING in Rome is a famous landmark of some sort. Unfortunately, both The Pantheon and Trevi Fountain were covered in scaffolding so we could only see them in a half-assed way. What many don't know is that the coins thrown in the fountain are collected every night and given to an Italian charity called Caritas. Caritas, in turn, uses the money for a supermarket program giving rechargeable cards to Rome's needy to help them get groceries. It's like their version of what we call Food Banks.

14 - FLORENCE, ITALY
Wednesday 3/29/1989

This morning, we packed quickly, had breakfast, and headed to The Termini to catch a train to Florence, the last stop on our study-tour. It took about three hours, and once we got to Florence, we all had to wait outside the train station until Dr. O'Neill came back after sorting things out with the hotel. Once again, it was hacky-sack time, and all the Italians who love soccer were just staring at us with intrigued smiles. What an icebreaker?! It transcends language barriers. Who would have thought? A little leather ball filled with tiny plastic beads that you pass to each other in a circle using only your feet.

We finally got to our rooms and unpacked. Szyd and I went out to the open-air markets that line the streets of Florence. I grew up around a lot of Italians in Chicago, afterall, being an Irish-Catholic we shared the same churches, the same schools, etc. So, I was familiar with the stories about Italian made leather, and how it was "the best" in the world. Now, I wanted a leather jacket for the longest time, but they were always too expensive. In Italy, leather was comparatively cheap to what we pay in America, so I was getting one.

I was operating throughout this whole semester on a finite budget of traveler's cheques without as much as an emergency credit card (this will be crucial later), so I couldn't spare the funds for an expensive purchase. I don't know how I did it, but I convinced Szyd to let me borrow his credit card for the leather jacket, and I would just pay him back at a later time. Szyd is a great guy! It was a brown leather jacket made of Italian sheepskin which is some of the softest made. I still have it to this day, but honestly, it is an "80s style".

At 5pm, Dr. O'Neill took the group on a tour of the city. We saw St. Lorenzo's which is the parish church built by the Medici Family of Florence for the city and, of course, themselves. We also saw The Duomo which means "dome" in Italian, and it's the Cathedral of Florence. It is built of white and green marble with a huge red dome at the transept. Relatively speaking, the interior is very plain, but it is huge. In front of the cathedral is a separate building called the baptistry which is famous for its frescoed ceiling. We also saw The Medici Palace, but it didn't seem as grand as it sounded, but then again, Florentine architecture is unique.

Upon returning from our field-trip, we had dinner in the hotel which was on Our College's tab. Thank God, because we were eating really good in Italy, but it was expensive eating out all the time. We needed to get back to going to the grocery store and buying foods that travel well without refrigeration.

Thursday 3/30/1989

This morning we left early with Bryce Vetter to the Pitti Palace which is where the Medicis lived. It was a very nice abode, but a little on the gaudy inside. That is one of the qualities of renaissance style. Their artwork was exquisite, but their architecture was a little behind.

The view from Piazza de Michelangelo

We walked up to the Piazza de Michelangelo, which is a big garden up on the side of a small mountain across the Arno River from the old town. It offers the best view of the city by far. Szyd and I saw some small gold hoop earrings in a store on the Ponte Vecchio which is a bridge spanning the Arno River. It's a famous bridge that has all kinds of gold and jewelry shops on it. Each of us had one pierced ear, and we wanted to buy them and split them. One earring for him and one for me, but we decided to wait. Florence was a shopper's paradise. I never got excited about shopping before I came to Florence.

For all Italy has going on for itself, the gypsies are a MAJOR drawback. While going through a market, somehow Szyd was pickpocketed to the tune of 70,000 Lire! That translated into about $47 in 1989 dollars! Needless to say, Szyd just stayed at the hotel that night. He was feeling a bit low.

Some of the rest of us went out for some Florentine entertainment. My run-in with the criminal element was yet to come this evening, though. On our way out, I saw a guy selling cassette tapes so I took a look. I was a little sick of my same old ones. I noticed a new Pink Floyd tape, "Delicate Sound of Thunder", and it was a great deal, so I bought it. It was even wrapped up in the heat-sealed cellophane that new cassettes came in, but when I unwrapped it, I found a TDK recording tape! I immediately went back looking for my money and hoping the SOB didn't pack up and run. When I found him again, the bastard all of a sudden didn't remember English anymore! That's when I got angry and wouldn't take my eyes off of him in case he ran. Apparently a multilingual person overheard the commotion. Then an arm comes over my left shoulder pointing a finger at him and hollering in a language I didn't recognize. It could have been broken Italian with a foreign accent, but all I knew was that I wasn't taking my eyes off of him. The crooked vendor finally relented. I got my money back and gave him his bootlegged tape. It turned out my hero was an Egyptian who spoke English and Italian as well. This was our second meet-up in Italy with friendly English-speaking Egyptians.

Friday 3/31/1989

This was a hang out day. Others went to more museums, but as for Szyd and I, were museum-ed out by this time. Instead we went to Ponte Vecchio, the bridge with the shops, to buy those earrings we saw the day before. 24 carat gold hoop earrings for

$16 US or $8 each for us. For the first time, Florence taught me that shopping actually can be fun.

Since we were already over the Arno River, we figured we'd go up to the Piazza de Michelangelo, the spot with the view of Florence, and play more hacky sack.

We accomplished about fuck-all today! We really needed to rest a bit, because we've been going, going, going for a long time, and we were about to embark on our own independent travels with our Eurail Passes, so we needed rest.

Saturday 4/1/1989

This was our "last day of class" in all practicality, and we were taking a day trip to Siena. It's a picturesque little Tuscan town, but it's hard to navigate because it's built way up on a hill. Siena was the home of the 14th century saint, St. Catherine of Siena.

The picturesque Tuscan village of Siena.

101

Of course, we saw their Duomo or "Dome/Cathedral". As with many of the old cathedrals in Europe, this one contains relics of saints as well. They have St. Catherine's head and one of her fingers. Don't ask me how they got there?

We went back to the hotel. Being the end of the semester, we had to take this time to finish up all of our loose ends with our schoolwork. No finals this time. It was also a social time, because everyone was saying their good-byes. We were a very mixed group of 26 students, many of which didn't know each other when we got there. But by the end of this semester, being away from EVERYTHING that is familiar to us, we became quite close. We were all each other had to cling to, and now we were all going to traverse across Western Europe in all directions in small groups.

15 - ARRIVEDERCI ITALIA
Monday 4/2

We were anxious to get on the road and today was actually a school free day, so we jumped on the 6:58am train from Florence to Bologna. "We" consisted of Szyd, Bryan and myself, as well as four other girls Kim, Kelly, Cheryl, and Karen.

At Bologna, we had to change trains. We caught the 8:46am for Lecce which let us off in the port city of Brindisi at about 5 or 5:30pm. We were hungry and got talked into what we thought was a tourist trap. This guy was American, and could probably make a fortune as a car salesman.

We took him up on it. Apparently, he was also a traveling college student who was a little down on his funds, and was waiting tables at this restaurant for the day until the ferry left. Anyway, it turned out to be a great deal as were most of the restaurants we encountered in Italy.

Our ferry was set to depart at 10:30pm, but didn't leave until 11pm. We'll find out the hard way about how the ferries, trains, and coaches all work together closely depending on what country you operate out of.

That night was pretty challenging. Our Eurail Passes only provided for passage on the deck of the ship. No seats inside where it was heated or anything like that, and the Adriatic Sea gets VERY chilly at night. We couldn't stand it anymore so we decided we had to find somewhere inside to sleep. Since the conductors were wise to us, we found the movie theater in the ferry and laid down in the rows. It was warm, and we were hidden from "Johnny Law" until morning.

Monday 4/3

When the sun came out it really warmed up, so we just hung out on the deck of the ship and got some color. The coasts of Yugoslavia and Greece are beautiful.

Italian ferries suck. I've seen cleaner bathrooms in corner taverns in Chicago scum neighborhoods. And naturally because it was an Italian ferry, it works with the Italian motorcoach lines running between Petras and Corinth. As a result, we watched our Greek train heading for Corinth depart the station as our ferry was docking. Hence, why the damned ferry left Brindisi, Italy a half hour late.

Petras is a port town on the northwest corner of the Peloponnesian Peninsula of southern Greece. Corinth, like the same town you've heard of in the bible, was at the northeast end of the same peninsula.

It was about 5 or 6pm. The next train wasn't until 2am, so we were sunk. We didn't know where to go or what to do. Out of nowhere, we met a very nice Greek man who spoke perfect English named George and his friend Saradis. They helped us lock up our bags at the railway station and promised us a good inexpensive Greek meal. We had nothing better to do, so we took him up on it.

This place was really off the beaten path and the street was less illuminated the farther we went. I was starting to wonder about our hospitable Greek hosts? Bryan, Szyd, and I walked in a triangle formation with the four girls in the middle, and I had my hand on the switchblade I bought in Italy.

Everything turned out to be great. It was a little Mom & Pop Shop with their food displayed in a deli-like showcase. No Greek boogey man. Ordering was kind of fun. Mom & Pop didn't speak a lick of English, and George's food vocabulary in English wasn't the best. I somehow decided that, if I make the noise of the animal that was sacrificed for the meal, she'd understand. So when I started Mooing or Clucking, it just made for good laughs and entertainment.

Anyway, we had a huge meal including bread, salad, and beers for about $3 US including a tip! A dollar went a LONG way in Greece in 1989. If I remember right, we were getting 157 Dracma for $1 US. A Gyros sandwich cost 90 Dracma, A 16oz. bottle of Lowenbrau brewed in Munich was 90 Dracma. We were going to live well in Greece, even on traveling college student budgets.

The trains in Greece are unique. The rest of the continent's trains run on a tight schedule you could set your watch to. This night, we caught our 2am train at 2:30am. This was just a prelude of what was to come.

16 - Hello Hellas!
Tuesday 4/4/1989

I was completely exhausted from constantly traveling without a good night's sleep since Florence two days ago. I just remember small farm animals on this train in the middle of the night. It was quite unpleasant.

Our train arrived in Corinth at 5am after many delays. It was too early to call my and Kim's friend from Chicago, Christos. We couldn't find a hotel or hostel cheap enough, so we opted to sleep in the train station with the bums. I was relegated to a luggage rack with slats to sleep on, so I stole a seat cushion from under a bum's feet. His feet wouldn't miss it, and the slats hurt my hip. I could use my bag for my upper body.

At about 7:30 am, I called Chris and he met us at about 8:30 am. He took us for tea at a nice sidewalk cafe, and later to his house. There we all took well needed showers, except there were 7 of us, and the hot water tank is only so big. The girls went first, and I was last, so I got an ice cold shower, but it felt good after what we'd been through.

Chris is an eccentric character, but an all-around great guy! You couldn't meet a nicer or more generous person during a long walk on a Sunday afternoon, and he sure showed that on our visit. Well anyhow, while the girls were showering and getting ready, Chris showed us his weapons. I think he's connected to the Greek mafia or some connection thereof. He had enough to hold off a small army for at least 20 minutes.

After we were all clean, Chris' wife made us a meal so big we couldn't even finish it all. It was a Traditional Greek spaghetti. It didn't have a red sauce like the Italian Spaghetti we're used to. It was more of a quasi-clear sauce where you could see the colors of the ground beef and spaghetti. Wow?! Was it delicious?!

Chris and I left the others to hang out so we could find a nice place for us to stay. He swindled us a deal at a nice hotel, not a hostel, that came to about $5-$6 US per person per night! Chris can sure work a deal. I love Greece!

When we lugged our bags over to the hotel, and the girls decided to take a nap. Szyd, Bryan, and I decided to go rent motor scooters. They were rented out for 24 hour periods of time. Again, the dollar went very far in Greece, and we paid pittance for these things. The three of us went all around modern (as opposed to ancient) Corinth and saw everything. That's when we needed to take a nap, and crashed out from 7pm-9pm. We got ready to go out with Chris, but somehow wires got crossed and had to meet up with him later. In the meantime, it was Gyros sandwiches for 60 to 70 cents US!

Wednesday 4/5

I had a flat tire on my motor scooter, so I had to push it back and get another one. I knew it was only the beginning of April, but the Greek sun sure was hot. Afterall, we came from Minnesota via England only a few months earlier.

We cruised around for a while and later took the girls to see Ancient Corinth in shifts. (3 scooters and 4 girls). Ancient Corinth is about 7 miles outside of modern Corinth. Going through the countryside, I figured there must have been a bee farm somewhere nearby, because I got hit with bees on my arms, forehead, and the scooter.

Courtesy of Matt Barrett's Greece Travel Guides

This is when my camera finally crapped out

Ancient Corinth was mind blowing. For someone who has a good sense of classical history, and some rudimentary architectural and mechanical knowledge, this was the ultimate place to be. It came in handy that we did have these knowledge prerequisites, because the Museum Workers were on strike, and there were no plaques to explain what you were looking at either. We figured out that they had central heating in their homes in Ancient Corinth through floor tiles heated with hot water running through channels under the floor. In 300-something B.C., who the hell would have thought?

We returned the motor scooters and got ready to meet Chris again. He took us out for a major feast! We had bread, cheese, salad, fries, awesome lamb, and beers galore. The Greeks serve their beers a little differently, but a good method, nonetheless. We were having 16oz bottles of Lowenbrau. They'd also give you a small 8oz glass to drink from. That way, the wait staff could keep cold bottles of beer on the table at all times, and no one has to ask for more beer. They just kept the bottles full.

Later on, we went to a bar that didn't sell beer, only spirits! What kind of bar is that?! That place was very interesting to say the least.

It was a bit of a Corinthian dive, so the girls didn't stay long. But, Bryan, Szyd, and I were staying because Chris was buying! Everybody was in a party mood that night. Especially the hooker who didn't speak a lick of English. Chris thought he'd be funny by telling her, in Greek of course, that Bryan, the tall one, really liked her. She saw a business opportunity right away and pounced. Americans with lots of money! Szyd and I were really enjoying seeing Bryan get mildly molested by this prostitute.

Somehow Bryan, in desperation, managed to overcome the language barrier and convince the hooker to go after Szyd. This was funny too, until Szyd managed to overcome the same language barrier and redirect her attention to me. I think that's when we did one more farewell shot and left.

Thursday 4/6

Today was the day we went to Athens, the cradle of modern Democracy! We got ready and just hung out most of the day. I figured out how to translate Greek to English, but it was a really drawn out process. I knew the Greek alphabet from pledging my fraternity, and I knew the sounds each letter made, as well as Greek/Latin word roots, or etymology. After going through this laborious process, I figured out the sign said Bank of Greece. I suppose I could have just as easily looked at the monetary exchange sign in the window.

We went to catch the 3pm train to Athens, which naturally came about 3:45pm. Athens was a rather polluted and smelly town. You could feel the polluted air on your throat. The smog was so bad that Athenians were only allowed to drive on the days that corresponded with your license plate number. Even numbered plates on even numbered days, and odd numbered plates on odd numbered days.

The only thing to really see in Athens is the Acropolis. Home of the Parthenon and the birthplace of Democracy. We walked, or climbed, up the Acropolis and struggled to find our way in. By the time we figured that out, it was closed for the night. So, we just walked around and saw some of the older parts of town.

We saw these cute girls that just finished eating in a basement restaurant. By now, I was all sunburned and had lost loads of weight from all of the walking. I'm feeling kind of confident in myself so I gave her the old baby blues and my best smile. I got a positive response, so I went down and sat at their table. After a bit of conversation, I found out that she was Linda Fox, the older sister of one of my fraternity brothers, Tom Fox! I almost fell off of my chair! What are the odds?! I finally got up the nerve to just walk up to a pretty girl and start talking to her, and she's "hands off". WTF?! Just my luck. Of course, we stopped for a drink and went back to the hostel.

Friday 4/7

We woke up early to leave in our laundry, because we hadn't had a stitch of clean clothing for quite some time now. Everything else in Greece was dirt-cheap, so we might as well pay someone else to do it for us. Besides, spending my day at a washeteria wasn't my idea of touring Europe.

We walked back to the Acropolis only to find that the guards and workers in all the museums and ruins were on strike on the only day we'd be in Athens. We had to keep moving, because Athens was really off the beaten path in Europe in 1989. It was at the bottom of a peninsula separated from the rest of Free Europe by the Communists, so we had to back-track all the way through Italy just to begin our next new adventures.

We made the best of our day though. We got some photos of the Parthenon from a distance. Hey, it proved we were there, but my camera finally crapped-out in Corinth from the drop in Swansea, Wales. This was unbeknownst to me until I got

111

back to Chicago in July. One thing we did see was the original stadium for the Modern Olympic Games. It's an open-air 1896 stadium that doesn't require admission or anything, but it sure was small. I've seen high school stadiums that were bigger.

We kicked back until our laundry was done, collected it, and caught the 3:45 pm train to Petras for the ferry. Our train got into Petras at 8:30 pm, and our ferry departed at 10:30 pm. This was the place where the boys and the girls departed, because seven is too big of a group to travel in unless you're on some guided tour.

Saturday 4/8

We woke up on the ferry, washed up, and said our farewells to the girls as our boat docked on the Island of Corfu about 8-8:30 am. Szyd, Bryan and I wanted to party on a Greek Island, and Corfu fit the budget.

Szyd had his copy of Fodor's "Let's Go Europe" which was our travel bible. There, we found a place called the Pink Palace on the west side of the island. This was basically a resort that traveling college students could afford. If I remember correctly, it was only about $23 US per person per night which included continental breakfast and dinner. We had a private room with two bunk beds and a private bathroom. There was a big jacuzzi the size of a small pool outside our room in the middle of a courtyard. Dinner was served buffet style on the veranda overlooking the Adriatic Sea while watching the sunset. We thoroughly enjoyed the sun, surf, jacuzzi, and of course the topless beaches. For Greece, this was conservative. Most Grecian beaches are totally nude.

That place was party central for traveling college students. They served Lowenbrau beer brewed in Munich for just under $1 US for a 16 oz bottle. It was more than we were paying in Corinth, but it was still dirt cheap, which was a fact we took advantage of.

The beach was a whole concept alone for Puritanical Americans. Having said most Greek beaches were totally nude, the Pink Palace was rather conservative. The girls out there were only topless. We loved the scenery, and I had my confidence up after meeting my fraternity brother's sister in Athens. We really wanted to talk to them, but how do you talk to a topless stranger and try to keep your eyes off of her boobs? "No, I'm really interested in you for your mind." Yeah, right! That was an obstacle we never overcame, so we didn't meet any cute girls there.

We called it an early night because the van to the other side of the island left at about 6am.

Sunday 4/9

We woke up about 11:30 am and had a rather mellow day that was well needed after all of the running around. It can get hectic. Besides, I was very sunburned by now and a bit hungover. I haven't been out for a good booze-up in a long time. My tolerance was down. It's always been a pint here and a pint there in Europe, so I got crocked rather easily.

We called it an early night because the van to the ferry on the other side of the island left at about 6am.

17 - Buongiorno again Italia
Monday 4/10

Our day began at 5am. When we first arrived on Corfu and got off the ferry on our way to The Pink Palace, we got a Mercedes taxi that was paid for us, but not on the way out. They piled 10 or 11 of us into the back of a VW cargo van for the trip over the mountain to the other side of the island to the ferry.

The ferry was scheduled to leave about 9:30 am, so we had a little time to browse at the Duty Free Shop. You didn't find Duty Free shops that often because most of the borders we crossed were open borders where you didn't even need to go through Customs in most cases.

At the Duty Free, we couldn't resist the tax free prices, let alone that this was Greece, and everything was dirt cheap in the first place. We were beer drinkers, but lugging a load of beer with us was impractical. In honor of our gracious host, Greece, we bought the national drink of Greece, Ouzo. It was the good stuff too "Ouzo 12" for only $2 US per bottle.

Our ferry arrived in Brindisi, Italy about 4:30 pm. We ate a meal and caught the 6:30 pm train INTENDING to get off in Bologna at 3:24 am.

On the train, the three of us were playing Spades. Games were usually a good way to meet people, but nobody understood the game much less English. After each hand was dealt, we passed a bottle of Ouzo around. The Italians must have thought we were nuts or something. But the more we played and drank, the more they became interested in our game. After a while, we had a crowd forming outside our couchette.

Well, the train rolled on through the evening. Bryan won, we closed the door, and lost our Italian audience. I set my reliable wind-up travel alarm clock in time to get off in Bologna at 3:24 am. This was an important train change, because we were intending to go behind The Iron Curtain where the "evil communists" lived and see Hungary so we needed to head northeast. The train we were on continued farther west towards France, and we didn't want to do that if we could at all avoid it.

Tuesday 4/11

I later woke up to Bryan grabbing my knee and shaking it saying, "Mike, Mike wake up! Where the hell do you think we are? It's 6:30!"

I checked my alarm clock, and some joker turned off the alarm, probably thinking he was funny, but we weren't laughing. We knew we were close to France, but we didn't want to go back there. We'd had enough rudeness to last a lifetime. Just then, we felt the train slowing down and decided to get off wherever we were and flip-flop back to the train hub in Milan.

In the commotion of getting our shit together as the train was slowing, Szyd forgot his contact lenses somewhere in the couchette. The poor guy was sunk. Now he had to wear his coke-bottle glasses until we got back home. It took him a while to get used to them, and he was tripping over tall curbs, stairs, and the like.

Disembarking from the train, we realized we were in the Italian town of Torino. At the time, we didn't realize that Torino was Italian for Turin. As in The Shroud of Turin that Jesus was wrapped in when he was buried. Wow! We blew that opportunity due to a language barrier.

So, we caught the train back to Milan which was a major transportation hub. We originally planned to go to Vienna, Austria to get visas at the Hungarian Embassy, but since we were that far west, we changed plans and went up to Switzerland first.

We caught the 9:20 am from Milan to Brig, Switzerland. From there we went to Bern, the Capital of Switzerland. I've never seen such a clean city in my life! I was actually impressed by a public restroom out in a public park. We left Bern that evening heading for Zurich where we got a room for the night. The problem was that we didn't have any Swiss Francs yet. Changing money from one country to the other was such a hassle. I've never done more in-my-head math at any other time in my life. This will become a funny issue for Bryan when we get to Munich, Germany.

18 - On Swiss Time
Wednesday 4/12

Thank God for the nice people at the Youth Hostel. Even though we didn't have any Swiss currency, they still put us up for the night with an IOU. When we woke up we ate breakfast, showered, and went to change money for our lodging while they held our bags as collateral. We checked out of the Hostel with our bags and checked them into the coin operated lockers at the train station.

Zurich was a whole lot bigger than Bern and also very clean. I've been seriously impressed by Swiss cleanliness standards and their standard of living. The Swiss were also very friendly. Some young school children saw us looking at a map and came right up to us to see if we needed help.

We had time to kill and didn't want to wander far from the train station because we were going to Vienna on the overnight train. Right next door to the station was the famous Needle Park. It's called that because in the middle of the park, there's the confluence of two streams thus making a needle shaped land figure where they meet.

The irony is that it's also the place where all of the junkies hung out. What was this? Switzerland had .2% unemployment at the time. I think they were all there in Needle Park.

Well, it had been a while since we smoked any hashish, Europe was rife with it, and we knew it. Switzerland was very liberal just like The Netherlands was, but it was not legal. Here the junkies sold "soft drugs" like hash in order to get money for their "hard drugs" like heroin. We also saw them coming across a footbridge each with a handful of clean syringes from the free clinic. The Swiss government did this for them to help stop the spread of HIV/AIDS. It seemed crazy at first, but it worked. They checked the spread of disease by providing clean needles to addicted junkies. It doesn't solve the addiction problem, but I guess they're fixing one problem at a time.

While walking through the park, one of the junkies asked us if we wanted to buy some hashish? I asked him what his "credentials" for selling hash were, and I was satisfied that he wasn't an undercover cop. We bought a little clump of Black Moroccan, and we were off on our way. The only problem was that we didn't have anywhere to smoke it. We'd have to wait until we got on the train and out of the station.

While in the station, we were just walking along, and out of nowhere, I heard someone holler "McEvilly"! Holy Shit?! I'm in the middle of a train station in Zurich, Switzerland traveling with the only two people I know right now, and I hear my name ring out. It's not like my name is common like Smith or Jones, but rather McEvilly! I mean, there were only 7 of us in the entire Chicago phone book growing up! We had a big freak out. It was Kim hollering my name. She saw my fraternity jacket with the skull and triangle on the back, knew immediately that there couldn't be two of those in Europe and just called out. She was still with Kelly, Cheryl, and Karen.

We thought we had lost them in Corfu, Greece, but I guess not. They were on their way to Vienna just the same as we were and on the same train. I forgot my cassette tape of Led Zeppelin's Physical Graffiti in Kelly's walkman in Greece. I thought great, I can get it back. WRONG!! She lost it! I was thoroughly pissed off, but there was nothing I could do except grin and bear it.

We found our own couchette away from the girls so we could stretch out the seats and sleep across them. We also wanted to smoke some of the hash we bought in Needle Park. We learned the patterns of the conductors on the train. If they already asked for your Eurail Pass once, they wouldn't bother you again. They also only came around right after the train left a new station. That being considered, we closed the drapes, turned off the lights as if we were sleeping, and smoked away with the window open wide. Wow, it was rejuvenating.

19 - AUSTRIA-HUNGARY EMPIRE
Thursday 4/13

I set my travel alarm to wake us up a little before we got to Vienna so we could freshen up. Again, we said our goodbyes to the girls and ventured off to find our "treasures". Wanting to lose each other was a pretty mutual feeling at that time, so it was easy.

We were on a mission to get to Budapest, Hungary because we wanted to see how the Communist Bloc lived, and this was the safest way to do it, so we went straight to the Hungarian Consulate to get visas. We were hoping to only have to spend a few hours in Vienna, but our visas would take until too late in the evening in order to get to Budapest that day.

We had to stay a day in Vienna which also meant another opportunity to change money again which also meant another opportunity to lose more money. Changing money is the biggest pain in the ass! Again, I've never done so much math-in-my-head in all :my life!

Vienna was a beautiful city, nonetheless. The architectural style and whole appearance of the place is very much like Paris. I wondered at the time if there was a correlation between these former cultural centers. I've since learned that, yes there was.

Marie Antoinette, the wife of the doomed Louis XVI of France, was from Vienna. Too bad she didn't stay there.

We managed to find cheap lodging at St. John Bosco parish hostel for men for 77 shillings. I think it was 13 shillings to a dollar or $6 US for the night.

Friday 4/14

The Consulate opened at 8:30 am, and our train left at 9:30 am. Of course, we got a late start at about 8:10 am. We had to take a bus and walk 20 minutes with our packs. We got our visas, and I ran around in the street trying to flag down a cab. We got to the station with 10 minutes to spare.

We still had the hashish we bought in Needle Park in Zurich and had to get rid of it. We smoked as much of it as we could in Szyd's sneak-a-toke the night before, but we still had some leftover. We tried to smoke it when we got on the train, but there were a lot of short stops and the conductor kept coming by, so we couldn't pull it out.

So the train starts slowing again, and the next thing you know, there's some 16 or 17 year old kid outside the train with an AK-47 in his hands and an officer next to him holding a German Shepard! Holy shit! We were at the Hungarian border already! The Iron Curtain! The Communist World! We had NO IDEA the Hungarian border was only 50 miles from Vienna, and we had hash in our possession!

The first instinct was to panic! Holy shit! Don't look panicked! They'll feed off of that. But, if they catch us, we'll be shoveling snow in Siberia at some Gulag for the rest of our lives! Holy shit!

Okay, maybe that German Shepard is just an attack dog and not a dope-sniffing dog? No, we can't take a chance. Put it in Szyd's toiletry bag, but now where do we stash the bag? Szyd's dirty laundry bag is ripe! Stick it in there and pray!

The officer was accompanied by a soldier. He had a grim look on his face like he wanted to chew you up from the knees down. He sternly barked "passport" in a variety of languages. When he saw the eagle on the cover of our passports, all fears subsided. He smiled and said, "Ah, Americans! Welcome to Hungary!"

I would have been a rich student if I just turned around and picked up the gold brick I just shit!

Every town we passed through had dirt streets and about 4 to 6 cars total. I've never seen such a dramatic socio-economic change by just crossing a border. It seemed the communists hadn't progressed at all since they took over at the end of World War II. Then again, it wasn't just a border crossing. It was the Iron Curtain, and we were behind it.

We got to Budapest about 1:30 pm, changed money, and found a place to stay. They didn't have the International Youth Hostel Association behind the Iron Curtain. Instead, there were private citizens who would rent out rooms from their own residences. We didn't know what or how or anything? Szyd's Let's Go Europe book was kind of useless in Hungary.

Arial Budapest from a postcard

We were lost until we found this nice lady who spoke very good English. The basis for going with her was that there was a minimal language barrier. She didn't even have a car, just a room in her flat to offer. We followed her home on the bus. The fare only cost 2 cents US, which was a foreshadowing for the rest of our time in Hungary.

We got settled at our hostess' flat and learned the ground rules. She was a very nice lady who worked really hard to make us happy. She had an a la carte menu of services to offer like laundry for 25 cents wash, 25 cents dry and fold. Breakfast was 25 cents too, and this is where I was first introduced to paprika on scrambled eggs. This lady was on her way to getting a tip!

This city was what Chicago must have been like in the 1940s and 50s. Little variety in the style of cars, minimal traffic, and NO COMPUTERS! My walkman broke, and I thought I could pick up a really cheap one here. We went to a top electronics store downtown to find one. The salesman who spoke English said that he'd heard of the walkman before, but they didn't

123

have them behind the Iron Curtain. Wow, this was becoming a Western Appreciation trip in a big way!

Since it was Friday, we decided to splurge at the "Rock Cafe" and pay 52 forints per beer when we were getting 58 for a dollar. After a few beers, we decided we need to finally get rid of the rest of our hash. It just wasn't safe behind the Iron Curtain. So, we went down to the shadows near the Danube River to finish it off. We saw the famous "Chain Bridge" and went under there to hide. As we were loading the sneak-a-toke, we noticed a small boat coming slowly downstream. As it got closer, I saw that it said POLIZEI or something to that effect. Either way, they were cops! Holy shit! Don't flick that lighter whatever you do! We just laid back down and didn't move a muscle or make a sound until the boat passed. If we had been found smoking that, this fantasy excursion we were on would come to an abrupt end! Lord knows we'd probably be shoveling snow in some Russian Gulag or something horrible for the rest of our lives. After that, we finished the hash and needed a beer!

The bridge under which we smoked hashish

We then somehow found an English Pub called Fregatt and finished our night there. We really had to unwind. Just thinking of the gravity of our situation was horrifying.

Saturday 4/15

We slept late and started off to see the sights. Budapest is an absolutely beautiful city, but it is an awful shame the way the Communists have taken care of it. For example, the Parliament building is a structure that was built somewhere around the 14th or 15th century with ornate gothic stonework. If over time a piece of this stonework art crumbles or falls off, they would repair it with plain red brick. That is, if they repaired it at all.

This was another one of those Western Freeworld appreciation lessons. In Western Europe, they would go to the ends of the Earth to find an artisan who could repair whatever it is that's falling into disrepair. So many places we went to had scaffolding set up all around the place. It obscured a lot of photos, but at least the West keeps up with regular maintenance.

Downtown was still historic and beautiful nonetheless, but outside the city center was a different story. I'd estimate that more than half of the sidestreets and minor roads were merely dirt and/or gravel. The private residence we stayed in was pretty much like the rest of the Communist World you saw on TV. Big block housing projects. The flat we stayed in was itself very nice, but the hallway smelled like the Primate House at the Zoo. Damn near everything was intimidating except the city center. That was very "westernized".

This westernization of Hungary is how and why Eurail Passes are honored here, and we're allowed to travel behind the Iron Curtain. There's actually a lot of competition in the Hungarian marketplace unlike many other Communist countries. The best part about it is that these guys must be rank amateurs at free-world economics. Their currency, the Forint, ain't worth shit, and a dollar goes a LONG way!

That night, we took a taxi home from the city center to get out where we stayed. It was easier than taking the bus and probably safer too. These neighborhoods all looked pretty dodgy. It only cost us about $2 US including a nice tip. He likes Americans now.

Sunday 4/16

We had to get an early start today because our train left for Salzburg, Austria at 4:25 pm. Again, we had to retrace our steps to get back to where we wanted to go.

The previous two days were cloudy and/or rainy, but today the sun came out, so we went up to The Citadella for the most beautiful view of the city. Budapest is actually two different cities that share a common name. We were staying on the eastern bank of the Danube River which is called Pest. The western bank of the Danube is Buda. Put them together and you get Budapest. While at The Citadella, we walked up the hill to Buda Castle and checked out the "old part of town" that dates back to the medieval times or God knows when.

In the old town, there were various horse drawn carriages. Well, I guess one of these stallions must have gotten an enticing view of some mare, because he was VERY excited. I've spent a lot of time on farms and around animals, but I've never seen anything like this! His erection was this monstrosity that emerged from the part that's still furry to extend to a length the size of my arm! All we could do was just stand there and clap to honor him and feel emasculated ourselves.

We were running late, so we took another taxi back to the flat where we stayed. What the hell, we felt like wealthy people for a few days. That ride only cost a little less than $2 US with tip. We grabbed our bags and said goodbye to our hostess. The taxi on the way back to the train station only cost about $1.50 US with tip. This place was great, but you can't change Hungarian currency outside of the Eastern Block, and it was Sunday so all the banks were closed. We were basically sunk. We just had to buy whatever we could with the Forints we had left before we got on the train. With limited choices at the station, we basically bought as many bottles of beer as we could carry and drank them on the way to Salzburg. Of course, we had to save a couple samples of this illegitimate currency for souvenirs.

We hopped on the train for Salzburg, Austria, but had to change trains in Vienna. We got to Salzburg a little past midnight. We were very exhausted and Bryan somehow mixed up the directions to the American Youth Hostel. We didn't get there and into bed until 1:30 am.

Monday 4/17

Today, Szyd and I took our time getting up, and Bryan took off on his own to see the town. Traveling is wonderful, but it is exhausting and will wear on your nerves from time to time.

Splitting up to tour a bit was probably a good idea. We've had a lot of togetherness lately.

Courtesy of a postcard

Salzburg is an absolute "fairytale town". The square where Mozart's home was located looked like you were walking through a child's pop-up book. Not only was the scenery and city beautiful, but also it's one of the first places I've seen in Europe without scaffolding.

Szyd and I also climbed up this small mountain to the Hohensalzburg Fortress which was amazing. I think this was the place where The Sound of Music filmed the scenes at the convent. I'd like to know how the hell they built that place way up there, much less get up that road in the wintertime?

At 2:30 pm, the American Youth Hostel showed The Sound of Music, which was filmed in Salzburg, on a big projection screen TV which was state-of-the-art in 1989. The idea was to watch the movie and then to go out and explore all the places they

128

filmed the movie. This movie has surely created a lot of tourism for this little picturesque town.

After the movie, they held a happy hour in the hostel's bar, which was really fun. The more people drank, the more the soundtrack of the movie was being sung. Somebody there knew of a good biergarten. It was called The Mullin Beer Gardens which used to be an old Augustinian Monastery. You'd get into a queue to get your beer that looked like a high school chow line. You'd rent your stein and then keep coming back to refill it. They didn't have the big beer-maids like you see on the St. Pauli Girl Beer label from West Germany, but I'd bet they save a load on having to clean a ton of glasses, not to mention the broken ones.

On the way home, we had to walk through the park where the Von Trapps sang "Do-a deer, a female deer, Re-a drop of golden sun, etc." So we couldn't resist. We were in the midst of dancing and singing that song when a couple of cops walked up. They knew we were drunk Americans and dispensed with their native tongue and the formalities just saying, "Go home!"

20 - WEST GERMANY
Tuesday 4/18

B ryan went off on his own again today. Togetherness all the time was starting to wear on us so Szyd and I just went off on our own too.

So, Szyd and I walked all over town and saw the rest of Salzburg. After watching the movie yesterday, we tracked down a number of the places where scenes from The Sound of Music were filmed.

We met Bryan at the train station around 7pm and we were on our way to Munich, West Germany. Remember, this was a time when East and West Germany were still divided. By the time we got to Munich, we were really Jonesing for some American food. We saw a Burger King and indulged ourselves. We were impressed at how well the cashier could speak English. Szyd ordered first with no hang ups, I ordered next without issue, but when Bryan ordered things fell apart a little. You see, we have changed money so many times in the past couple of weeks that you can't barely keep track of it all. Traveling students today have it made with the Euro standard through most European countries. Bryan handed her some money, and most of it was foreign currency. She even recognized the Hungarian Forint he handed her, and she reminded him that they're not allowed on this side of the Iron Curtain.

We checked into the youth hostel and stored our bags. We then went down to the Hofbrauhaus which is a big tourist beer hall in the "old city". It wasn't that great because it was filled with out-of-line Italians from Naples who were there for the soccer game tomorrow night at Olympic Stadium. They were loud, obnoxious, and couldn't handle their drink. Sloppy drunks.

The Old City and Cathedral in Munich
Courtesy of a brochure

Wednesday 4/19

Today, we did a walking tour of Munich through the Old City and the Walking District. This city has some beautiful buildings from its past but they aren't authentic like they once were. The Allies did quite a number on Germany during World War II and much of Munich was destroyed. After seeing all of the centuries old buildings in other countries, you can tell that there's been a lot of repairs done. But unlike behind the Iron Curtain in Hungary, the Germans at least repaired for posterity sake what was damaged. Prost!

The drunk Italians we saw at the Hofbrauhaus last night were at it again. This time in the Marienplatz outside of City Hall. They were waving flags, jumping around, and singing stupid-assed songs with no real words all day long, literally.

In some youth hostels, you can sleep a little late or at least hang out there for a little while, but in West Germany, they want you up and out early. Lock-out time was at 9am, so we called it an early night, not to mention, we had had enough of the drunk Italians.

Thursday 4/20

Today was going to be a momentous day. We were taking a day-trip outside Munich to a town called Dachau. It was the scene of the first Nazi Concentration Camp in 1933 which started Hitler's Final Solution on its way to almost becoming reality. EVERYONE regardless of your background should someday see a Nazi concentration/death camp. It would be one of the most moving experiences you will ever have.

On the way there, Szyd, Bryan and I met a nice young couple from New Hampshire who were in Europe on business. Mark and Donna noticed my fraternity jacket, because Mark used to hang out with all the guys from my fraternity when he was in college. The trip to Dachau was all nice and lively, but it was no foreshadowing of what we were about to see.

These are the gates at Auschwitz, but they were all the same essentially.

We were all greeted with a small pamphlet that contained an apology to the world for what occurred there. That the citizens of the town of Dachau didn't really know what was going on in there, and when they did, they tried to kidnap the Jews out of the fields when they were doing forced labor. Whatever? We weren't stopping in that town to give them any of our tourist money.

What was going through my head was that I was walking on the same ground that Satan himself must have lived on for those 12 years from 1933-1945.

The officers' barracks, now a museum

You first went through what used to be the officers barracks. They were now converted into a museum where they presented photos and actual documents used to force the Jews into Dachau translated into 4 different languages. The barracks were silent for the most part except for the occasional wail and the sound of a thud when their knees hit the floor. The overwhelming sadness in the room was palpable.

Next, we went out to what looked like a parade ground. I guess this is where all of the Jews would muster for announcements, roll call, or whatever. To the right, there was a long row of prisoner barracks. They were awful. Bunks slammed together with a bunch of 2X4s, and they were cramming 3 people into each bunk by the time things were going bad for the Nazis.

We walked out back to a brick building with a very tall smokestack. I had a feeling I knew what we were heading for. I was right. That was the ventilation for "The Ovens". They were

134

hideous. Big swinging iron doors with a platform on sliding rails going into the oven. People were awestruck. Still, there was no idle conversation among the visitors.

The next building housed the gas chambers. This was a particularly hard part of the death camp to see. The door to the gas chamber was a big, thick metal door that looked like it was on a walk-in freezer. On the inside, the walls were all laid with bathroom tiles, and there were shower-heads coming out of the walls. Maybe it was psychosomatic, but I thought I smelled "death" in there. I've never smelled a decaying body before, but that chamber had a smell that I don't think I've ever smelled before. And don't want to smell again.

I walked out of the gas chamber feeling completely emotionally drained, took a left into an empty room, and just stared out the window in disbelief of what I had seen. The window looked out onto the parade ground I mentioned before, and I noticed a black and white photo to the upper right of the window. The photo was of the window I was looking out, but that wasn't all that was in it. Piled as high as I am tall, were emaciated naked corpses from the gas chamber I just saw!

That was it! I'd had enough emotionally! I went outside and slid backwards down the wall crying!

The last thing to see was a huge memorial at the very back end of the camp. It was dedicated not only to the 6 million Jews who were systematically murdered during the Holocaust, but also the 4 million Poles, and 2 million Gypsies also systematically murdered. We CAN NEVER FORGET or else it will all happen again.

Compliments of the Hofbrauhaus

We had a bite and a couple of beers and caught the train back to Munich. On the way back, we met up with Megan (the girl who dropped and broke my camera in Swansea, Wales), Donna, and Katie. We arrived too late in Munich for the train to our next destination so we all decided to go to the Hofbrauhaus for one or two.

On the way to our next train, I realized that I forgot my newly bought walkman at the Hofbrauhaus. I ran back to get it, but that caused us to miss our second train. Thank God that in Western Europe, the trains run day and night all the time, so we finally caught the third train heading for Amsterdam via Innsbruck.

Friday 4/21

We got into Amsterdam at about 9:30 am and went straight to Bob's Youth Hostel. This is where Szyd and I stayed when we came here last February. Bryan soon realized that he made a mistake by going to Edinburgh with everyone else instead of Amsterdam with me and Szyd back then.

We were taking a well needed break from all of the going, going, going and decided to go off of our intended route. We also learned how to save money by taking long overnight trains. We found out early about how to manipulate a couchette to meet our needs. A couchette is a little passenger compartment with three seats facing three. The seats recline, but if you pull them out hard enough, they'll lay flat and meet with the fully reclined seat on the opposite side. Perfect for the three of us! Before we hopped on a train, we'd walk along the platform looking for an empty couchette then jump on that car. Once inside, we'd store our bags, pull the curtains, turn off the light, pull out the seats, and act like we were sleeping. Other passengers would just go past. Once the train pulled out of the station, we'd sit up and turn the lights back on until it was time to actually crash out.

Anyway, we checked our bags at Bob's Youth Hostel and went out on the town. We weren't interested in history or culture that day. We just wanted to relax, blow off steam, and show Bryan what a modern-day Sodom and Gomorrah looked like.

Of course, we went to a coffee shop first. These things were institutions of this city and an integral part of its culture. When you walk into a coffee shop and have a seat, they'll naturally hand you a menu. But, this menu lists the house specialty, Marijuana and Hashish. We weren't really interested in any more hash and went with our old standard of buds. The menu listed things like Jamaican, Maui Wowie, Filipino, Thai, the whole nine yards. It was all a standard price of 25 Guilders. What varied was the amount of buds you got depending upon its potency: 2.0g for basic Sensimillia, 1.8g of Jamaican, 1.6g of Thai, etc. Even the napkin holders were interesting. They had an additional little U-shaped compartment to dispense rolling papers. Nothing was left to chance. They even had your choice of Space Cakes at the register on the way out.

Saturday 4/22

Today, we decided to check out a bit more of the city because Bryan hadn't been there before. At one point during the day, we kind of got lost and were just wandering aimlessly. We realized after a while that we wandered into the wrong part of Amsterdam. It seemed that we were in some run-down warehouse area. This was all looking as dodgy as hell. As we walked a little farther, we realized that there were squatters or homeless people watching us, and we had to get the hell out of there. We made our way back to civilization quickly and decided to pay more attention to the map, Especially when we're wandering around all buzzed and everything.

That evening, we got back onto our intended route and caught the overnight train back to Munich. We were heading for Schloss Neuschwanstein near Fussen. Or in other words, The Original Disney Castle in Bavaria.

Sunday 4/23

We arrived back in Munich and caught another train to the town of Fussen. Our big problem was again, changing money. Today was Sunday, we forgot to get Deutschmarks ahead of time, and everything was closed. We did manage a bit of luck though. We found a hotel that changed our money without totally taking advantage of us.

This was another one of the castles or fortresses that makes me wonder, how the hell did they make that? I know Kaiser Ludwig II nearly broke the Bavarian coffers building it in the 19th century, but he was crazy anyhow, for real.

Schloss Neuschwanstein
Photo courtesy of the Bavarian Palace Administration

After the Disney Castle, we wanted to venture into the Black Forest. We heard Freiburg was the gateway to the Black Forest, but it was awkward to get to because the Black Forest was between here and there. We had to go around it to get to Freiburg.

On the way there, we had a stop in Augsburg, and we wanted to change from one railcar to another. We couldn't get through the pass-thru door, so we jumped off the train to go to the next car. Right when we did that, the train started moving. I tried to jump back on the train and the conductor pushed me off as I was trying to get on again. Schmuck! I'm sure he understood Yiddish. It might also be the same word in German, prick.

Oh well, the three of us got stranded for an hour. We probably played Hacky Sack or something to keep ourselves busy. Hacky Sack was a crucial time killer while traveling Europe. As I've often said, games are a good way to meet people when you're abroad. Hacky Sack really seemed to appeal to Europeans. All I could figure is that it must be the eye-to-foot coordination necessary to play soccer. Wherever we were, if we had to kill time, we'd pull out the hacky sack. It almost always proved to be a social situation, language barrier or not. Well, we eventually made it to Freiburg, found a hostel, and crashed out.

Monday 4/24

We went into Freiburg, the Gateway to the Black Forest, and saw a few sights on the way to the railway station. This was a smaller gauge of a rail line and reminded me of light-weight commuter rail. Anyway, we found our way eastward to Titisee deep in the Black Forest which was highly recommended. This was a very small town, and we went hiking on a path away from the picturesque lake and into the hills to hopefully catch a good view.

Before returning to our hostel in Freiburg, we stopped at a beautiful Black Forest deli surrounded by huge evergreen trees and a stunning view of a crystal blue lake to grab a bite and a brew. While we were dining al fresco, we noticed a guy sitting alone who was obviously American. We could pick out other Americans at a distance by now. Anyway, we said hello and struck up a conversation. It turns out he was a colonel stationed in Stuttgart, Germany just north of where we were. He had some free time, so he signed out a motorcycle from the motor pool and went for a cruise through the Black Forest. Didn't sound like a bad day off at all.

We got back to Freiburg and got our bags from the hostel. Bryan wanted to go to see West Berlin, but you had to pay out of pocket for that. You had to cross a long section of East Germany to get to West Berlin, and I was running low on funds. So, Szyd and I bid farewell and happy trails to Bryan.

Szyd and I were headed for Strasbourg, France. We heard through the travelers' grapevine that there actually were Frenchmen who drank beer, so we thought we'd give France another chance. There must have been something going on in town that day, because we couldn't even find a place to stay, so we made a radical decision and headed for Copenhagen, Denmark. We always wanted to see the fabled "Christiania".

So, we hopped on another overnight train, but we didn't sleep well because we had to change trains in Frankfort and again in Hamburg. Copenhagen is on an island, so the railcar we were on went on and off of ferries on our way, and we got to Copenhagen a little past noon on Tuesday.

21 - COMING TO THE CLOSE
Tuesday 4/25

The first place in Copenhagen we headed for was the tourist info office to find a hostel, and most importantly, a shower because I haven't had one since Saturday. I was getting ripe. The public transportation system in Copenhagen sucked because you couldn't scam it. They had normal buses where you pay the driver as you get on, as opposed to having conductors who got on and off the buses checking and selling tickets. They made us honest.

We walked around and saw a bit of the town. The famed Tivoli Gardens looked impressive, but it was too expensive to go inside. But never fear, Christiania is near.

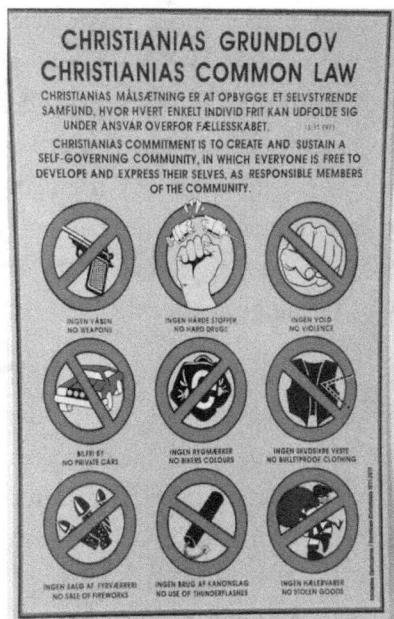

Courtesy of Wikipedia. The view when walking into Christiania.

Close to Tivoli Gardens was the infamous Christiania Commune. Our classmates back in England, Ijaz and Riaz first told us about this place and how we had to see it. Many years ago, some hippies took over, or occupied, a few square blocks and its run-down buildings in a central Copenhagen neighborhood. For some reason, (I don't know the whole story) the hippies declared that they were a sovereign autonomous commune and independent. The government apparently just accepted it, and here we are today. People selling hashish on the corner holding up a hunk of Black Moroccan Hash the size of a jumbo Hershey Bar. The drug trade here is completely out in the open and extremely rampant.

As long as we were tourists, we decided to explore this world that kind of looked like something out of Mad Max. It was a combination of that along with people dressed in what could be considered medieval garb. That was the way European hippies dressed. They didn't do the tie-dye and cut-offs like American hippies do. We walked into this huge courtyard that was surrounded by other buildings. There were people going about their business just like it was any other neighborhood.

We came across what appeared to be a bar and went in and ordered a round from a guy who had a case of individual bottles on the floor. Recently in Copenhagen, the bars here in Christiania were closed down because they operated tax-free and were giving other merchants unfair competition. That kind of explained the unspoken tension that was in the air when we walked in. We were outsiders so they were naturally suspicious of us. Well, we slammed that beer and got the hell out of there. I was definitely NOT feeling safe. On our way out, a few of the guys slowly followed us to the edge of Christiania to make sure we left.

After that, we saw a peculiar occurrence in central Copenhagen, rush hour. It wasn't that there's anything special about rush hour, but there were more bicycles than there were cars. They had special lanes for bikes and they were big ones. We noticed that the ladies pedaling those bikes in their business skirts and dresses all seemed to have nice shapely legs too. Not too shabby for rush hour.

That night, we just hung out at the hostel. There was a pond outside it, and we went out to watch the sunset on a clear night. Just then, I looked at my watch and noticed it was 9:45 pm. The sun was still up!? In April!? What's up with that?! I then looked at my map and realized that Copenhagen was the farthest north in the world I've ever been.

Wednesday 4/26

Today, Szyd and I realized we have very few Danish Krones left, and the commission charge was too much to change more money, so we decided to bail out of Denmark. We had Deutschmarks left from hitting West Germany twice, so we caught the first possible train back there. We came into Hamburg where we could at least get some food with the proper currency. We had 6 or 7 hours to kill in Hamburg, and there wasn't a lot to see because most of it was destroyed in World War II. In that case, we just drank a bunch of duty free beers that we bought on the ferry from Copenhagen back to the mainland.

The next train was overnight, so we woke up in Bruges, Belgium the next morning.

Thursday 4/27/1989

Upon arrival in Bruges, we walked across town to the Bauhaus where we stayed. We got ready and wandered around the town. In Bruges, there aren't any singularly famous attractions to see. The thing is to take in the town as a whole. Bruges is a town that was almost perfectly preserved because the big canal that connected it with the North Sea grew over and dried up due to the development of Zeebruges, or Bruges-by-the-sea. The town was economically ruined, but it helped preserve history.

Szyd and I stayed in a room with one guy from Toronto and another from Los Angeles. They were pretty cool guys, so we all went out for a few beers that night. Belgian beers are pretty tasty.

Friday 4/28/1989

We saw a bit more of Bruges today, and then caught the 3pm train for Amsterdam…for the 3rd time since we arrived in Europe! We lucked out by going back when we did, because the next day was Queen Beatrix's birthday. The whole place was set up for a major bash!

Our old standard, Bob's Youth Hostel, was full up, no vacancies. Referring back to Let's Go Europe, we decided on the Hotel Kabul for $1 more per night. It was located in the heart of The Red Light District, but it was a lot nicer.

At the hotel, we met up with a guy and a girl from Sydney, Australia. We had a night of major proportions! To start out, there was a band playing at the hotel, so we hung out there for a while jamming out. Later, we still had an appetite for music, so we went to the Hard Rock Cafe on the Leidseplein, a big entertainment center.

Saturday 4/29/1989

We checked out of the Hotel Kabul and went to the train station to check our bags. Normally, we would have just paid for a locker, but they were all taken. Because of all the revelers in town for the Queen's birthday, the train station set up a secure

146

room where we could check our bags. Too bad the queue for it had to be about 50 yards long.

We just basically just hung out to unlax and rewind. We had been on the road galavanting around Europe and living out of our bags for over a month, and I was tired. Besides, there was plenty of "people watching" to do. It was Amsterdam on the Queen's birthday, and all of the freaky people were coming out of the woodwork.

It also gave us time to say our farewells. Szyd and I have basically been together everyday since we first arrived at Gatwick Airport in London last January. We were good friends before back at school in Minnesota, but now we were very close and were going to be lifelong friends. Szyd's train left for Liege, Belgium at 2:15 pm where he was going to visit his uncle, then to London and back to America. I also had an uncle to visit, but he was in Ireland and I still had a long journey ahead of me. Whoa, I didn't know half of what awaited me on what I thought was going to be my way to Ireland, which was kind of like my second home.

After Szyd left, I found myself traveling solo for the first time. I'm a very gregarious person so this would be weird. I wandered around the packed streets of Amsterdam aimlessly. I really didn't have a goal or destination and funds were running low. The streets were so packed that no public transportation of any sort was running. What would have normally been a 15-20 minute walk from the train station to The Leidseplein took me over an hour through the crowd. Even though The Leidseplein was one of the "places to be", I thought that since it took me an hour to get here, I probably shouldn't wander too far from the train station. So, I went back and just hung out alone until my train left for Paris at 10:15 pm.

This ride sucked! I didn't have Szyd and Bryan with me to commandeer a couchette we could call our own. The train was also packed. I got stuck in a couchette with four Asians, a Spaniard, and a French woman none of whom spoke English. If that wasn't bad enough, I slept sitting up. Changing trains in Paris was crazy regardless of the time of day. Gare du Nord, the main train terminal in Paris, is the busiest one in Northern Europe.

Following directions from the girl at the Information Office in Amsterdam, I continued on my way to the harbor town of Cherbourg, France which is located at the western end of where the Normandy Invasion took place during World War II. This would be my last stop on the continent. From here, the plan was to sail on the ferry to Rosslare, Ireland. From Rosslare, I would take the train across the country to Westport, Co. Mayo. and stay with my Uncle Pa on our family farm.

I was down on my funds as I only had one 50 pound traveler's cheque left in the world. I didn't have an emergency credit card or any kind of safety net with me. I had to get to my family's village of Lettferbrock in Co. Mayo so I could work on my uncle's farm and earn money to get back to London, where the majority of our stuff was stored at the Kent's house. I also left a couple hundred pounds with Mrs. Kent for her to hold for safekeeping, just in case…well that case was about to rear its ugly head.

22 - CHERBOURG-MAY 1989

The downhill walk down to the harbor from the train station told the whole story before I had even gotten a chance to ask any questions. I had a bird's eye view of an empty harbor. The only ship left was one of the P&O Line Ferries on its way to Portsmouth, England. My Eurail Pass didn't work in Britain or any of its commuter lines to or from.

A deep feeling of deep dread set in.

I had nothing else I could do except see if I could find some help from the people with the P&O Line. At least, they spoke English.

The whole reason I got into this predicament in the first place is that I got bad directions in Amsterdam. I went to the information office at the rail station in Amsterdam to get some help on how to get to Ireland from there. Uncle Pa was expecting me in Letterbrock, our family's village outside of Westport.

Well, when it was Queen Beatrix's birthday, everybody and his brother was partying in the streets. Maybe at work too? Because the girl at the information office must have mixed up "Saturday" and " Sunday" in English and transposed them. I received instructions to arrive in Cherbourg on Sunday to catch a ferry to Rosslare, Ireland. WRONG!!! The damn thing left on Saturday and the next ferry wasn't until the next Saturday! I was out of time on my Eurail Pass which didn't work on British travel lines, I was out of food, and most importantly almost out of money. I didn't even have a credit card for emergency situations, and this sure as hell qualified as one!

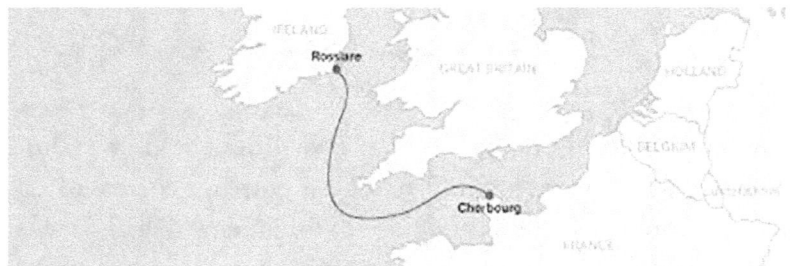

My original path to Ireland that got diverted to Portsmouth, England

So as I'm wandering my sorry ass down to the wharf, dreading what lies ahead with every step, I notice lights on in the P&O Line office. I asked them about my options, and they were grim. The only thing to do was to get onto the only ferry in the harbor and go to Portsmouth. I had to get to London. Uncle Pa would be worried waiting in Ireland, but he'd have to wait.

The crossing was long. About 5 hours if I remember correctly. I had only one £50 traveler's cheque left to my name. Thank God I left money with Mrs. Kent back in England for when I made it back.

The people at the P&O office couldn't change money, but they could give me the currency equivalent of what was printed in the day's newspaper. That was all nice and good until I realized they could only give change in Francs because we were in Cherbourg.

This was the type of ferry that saved me from the Normandy shores

Now, I had to change money AGAIN. This time on the ferry. Every time one changes money in Europe, one loses money! I was in a financially critical situation. Getting back to London depended upon the pittance I had left in my pocket, and it wasn't looking good. All I could do was gather myself for what was going to be a long journey home.

But where was "home"? I guess home at this point, it was my cousin's flat in Southgate, London. But, where the fuck was that?! I was only there once. Like, I was going to remember? I was in a bad way.

Meanwhile on the ferry, my crisis rolled on as I realized that I barely had enough for train fare back to London after the ferry docked in Portsmouth. I was just sitting at a table in the lounge feeling kind of low, when a fellow walked up to me and said something to the effect of, "Hey mate, are you alright? You look like you just lost your best friend?" That was my Guardian Angel, Pete Scawthorn. A "Bobbie" from Sheffield, England.

I said no, I hadn't just lost my best friend, but I was down on my luck. That was when Pete invited me over to a table where his family was sitting. The Scawthorn family were a very friendly bunch who were on holidays to Normandy, and they were on their way back home to Sheffield.

I told Pete my plight, and he took pity on me right away. He ordered up a meal of Bangers & Mash and a pint of Guinness for me. Pete was happy to help an American whose grandfather fought side by side with his father against the Hun. Well, who was I to disagree with him? During World War II, my father was a farmer boy in Ireland, and I was hungry. How could I refuse?!

His family and I sat around and talked and laughed for quite some time which helped shorten a 5 hour ferry trip. Pete wrote down his name, address, and phone number and invited me to come by his house in Sheffield… which, regretfully, I never did.

I did, though, call Pete 20 years later on Easter Sunday 2009. I could tell his family was a bit confused by the call, but when I told him the story, he recalled it. I told him he was my guardian angel, and I just wanted to thank him all these years later. I think I heard tears through the phone.

I didn't want to wear out my welcome, so I wandered around the ferry for a while until I found another friendly stranger with whom I had something in common. Emma Pascoe was an attractive British socialite whose father had a second house in either Barrington or Barrington Hills, IL. which is only about a 30-45 minute drive from where I lived. It's also where Walter Payton from the Chicago Bears and other famous people lived. Either way, she came from BooKoo bucks, but she wasn't stingy. I hung out with her for the remainder of the trip to Portsmouth, and she bought me a few pints along the way. Again, this was another friendly person on this ferry who offered me comfort and her phone number in America, but I regretfully never called.

Now in Portsmouth, my odyssey to London continues. I need to catch a train but I only have a few quid left. Thank God, I had enough for the fare, but I only had £1.51 left. No drinks or snacks on this leg of the trip because I'll still need Tube fare when I arrive in London.

This occurred very late at Waterloo Station, but I was still in time for the last train leaving central London. I had to get to Southgate, so I went to the automatic fare machine since there was no one around. The fare to Southgate was 1.50!! I think I've made it back home with one penny to spare, but I still needed to find my way from the Tube Station to my cousin's flat. My older cousin Breege and her husband Steve had a house in the Southgate area too which would become my permanent digs, but there was no way I could remember how to get there with the winding roads they have here.

I remembered that Fidelma, my cousin who's 2 weeks older than I am to the day, shared a flat with 2 roommates just up the hill and around the corner to the right, so I went for it. I really had no other choice. When I arrived, thank God there was a light on. Apparently, the pubs had just closed and they were hanging out before bed. Grainne, one of Fidelma's roommates, answered the door but didn't recognize me because I had run out of razors a week or two earlier, and I had substantial growth on my chin. When I opened my mouth, she immediately recognized me and welcomed me in. Unfortunately, Fidelma wasn't home. She was taking a long weekend down by the coast in Brighton.

I crashed hard there that night since I had basically been traveling for about 48 hours straight. In the morning, Grainne gave me directions to Breege and Steve's house where I would live for the next few months until my return home to Chicago.

If you want to do something amazing, see something amazing, or even achieve your wildest dreams, you're going to have to go beyond the horizon and venture into the unknown. While the pomp in that sounds glorious, fluffy, and boisterous, the reality is that it's true. You'll never see the world by staying in "Mayberry".

SPECIAL THANKS TO:

ROBERT SZYDLOWSKI

KIM HAND

KAITIE CARMODY

MAUREEN CARMODY

JIM FARNSTROM

SUSIE MCGUIRE

ARTHUR GATELY

DR. O'NEILL WHOSE ASSIGNMENT
MADE THIS BOOK POSSIBLE